Improve Your Gardening with
Backyard
Research

Improve Your Gardening with
Backyard Research

by Lois Levitan

 Rodale Press, Emmaus, Pa.

Printed in the United States of America on
recycled paper, containing a high percentage
of de-inked fiber.

Illustrations by Lois Levitan, Tom Gutekunst,
and Ed Courrier.
Designed by Jerry O'Brien.

**Library of Congress Cataloging in
Publication Data**

Levitan, Lois.
    Improve your gardening with backyard research.

    Bibliography: p.
    Includes index.
    1. Gardening—Experiments. 2. Gardening—
Research. I. Title.
SB454.L38   635'.0 724   80-13906
ISBN 0-87857-306-2 hardcover
ISBN 0-87857-267-8 paperback

2 4 6 8 10 9 7 5 3 1 hardcover
2 4 6 8 10 9 7 5 3 1 paperback

Contents

Before researchers become researchers they should become philosophers. They should consider what the human goal is, what it is that humanity should create.

Masanobu Fukuoka in The One-Straw Revolution

Introduction

So you like to garden.

And you probably receive lots of seed catalogs in the mail and read the columns on gardening that appear in your local newspaper, maybe subscribe to a gardening magazine or two and, perhaps, also have a few books on the subject sitting on your bookshelves. All of them chock full of advice.

Advice . . . advice . . . advice. Some of it suggests one thing and some of it says just the opposite. Most all of it is very good advice . . . for someone. But not all of it turns out to be good advice for *you*.

Why is that? It is simply because your garden and your gardening style are unique. You can't expect your work glove to fit perfectly on someone else's green thumb. Likewise, not all the suggestions you get on how to manage a garden are appropriate for your situation.

So, if you are the inquisitive sort who is curious about what is going on in your garden, but have found that you can't always rely on what others say, what do you do?

You can poke around, investigate what is going on behind the garden scenes, then look closely at the soil, the climate, the soil animals and fungi, the insect community, the seeds, and then at the plants. As a serious gardener you may have been doing something along these lines for years. But there is a special quality to poking around systematically by doing a scientifically valid experiment. When you have completed a project, you can draw a conclusion from it that will take some of the guesswork out of your gardening; your garden will be all the better for it.

Sure it takes some time and energy to carry out an experiment. You will probably find that you won't be able to do as many experiments as you have questions to answer. That is what other people are for. That is why books full of advice are written. Once you better understand how your garden works and how researching works—its potential and its limitations—you will be in a better position to take some of that advice and put it to good use.

With research you can find out not only what works best but why it works best. When you do an experiment and find out *what* is most successful under a particular set of conditions, you can apply these findings only to similar situations. If you know *why* a certain treatment has worked well, however, this knowledge can be used in any number of circumstances to help you make wiser decisions in your gardening.

This book is designed to help you become a credible researcher so that you can deal with the questions that your gardening, farming, and environmental interests raise and so that you can have confidence in the answers you come up with. It will not be telling you how to garden, but how to find out how to garden.

Being better informed won't diminish your awe or your excitement about gardening. If anything, your sense of wonder will increase as you become more aware of all there is in your garden to wonder about.

PART I

GETTING READY
TO DO RESEARCH

1

What's an Experiment?

THE SPINACH SAGA

(A play in one brief act; set in a garden, late in June. Two gardeners are talking.)

"Let me tell you about this spinach: it's fantastic—tastes better than any I've ever had!"

"Oh, yeah?"

"It's a new variety I thought I'd experiment with—called Green Thunder—and, I tell you, compared with what I've been growing, it's a much better producer. Just look at these big green leaves and at how thick it's come up. I'll bet every one of the seeds I put in germinated."

"Yeah?"

"Taste it. Go on, just pull off a leaf and eat it. Out of sight, isn't it? Really, without question, I'd recommend you use this variety in your own garden."

"Hmmm. . . ."

"Fact is, I'm sorry I didn't grow more of it myself this year. Actually I didn't plant much spinach at all. Most of the seeds I had left from last year got wet, so I couldn't use them. Nevertheless, I decided I would only buy a small packet of the Green Thunder variety because I hadn't tried it before. I didn't want to go hog-wild over it since I was just experimenting."

"Oh."

"Anyway, the garden's a lot smaller this year than it's been the last few years. Decided it wasn't worth having a huge garden if I couldn't care for it right. Funny thing is, I'm getting just about as much stuff out of this smaller plot as I was getting from the bigger one before."

"Really?"

"Yup, it's true. And since I didn't have to dig up so much for the garden this year, I've even had time to keep ahead of the weeds."

"That's something!"

"Then this friend of mine called last fall and asked if I'd clean the manure out of his chicken house. You've never seen so much and neither had I! Didn't know what to do with it all, so I composted it and even added some rock phosphate to the pile. This spring I dug all that compost into the garden."

"Oh, yeah?"

"And it sure made a difference. Just look at how well everything is doing. And, like I've said, I'm tickled pink about the results of my experiment with this new kind of spinach!"

"But . . . but . . . how do you know if the spinach has produced so well because of this new variety you used or because of all the fertilizing and fussing you've done?"

"Hmmm . . . well, I mean, well, I guess, um, well, gee, I don't really know for sure. But I tell you, I've never had such good spinach . . . reminds me of what spinach *used* to taste like. . . ."

The End

Ah yes, *The Spinach Saga* tells a tale of grand adventure in gardening, but does this an experiment make?

Well, we really can't draw any valid conclusions from the experience since, in addition to using Green Thunder for the first time, the gardener also weeded more, applied more fertilizer and soil conditioner, and purchased new seeds rather than planting those held over from previous years under dubious conditions. Even if the gardener's practices had not varied from his norm, the weather that season may have been particularly favorable for a spinach crop of any variety or it may have been an off-year for the spinach leaf miner. Without another variety of spinach grown alongside Green Thunder for comparison, we will never know precisely why it produced so well that fateful summer.

Although there was a *correlation* between the use of the new variety and the production of a bumper crop, we do not know if Green Thunder was the *cause* of the success. To find out, we would have to do a "controlled experiment" where at least two varieties of spinach are grown in plots [1] alongside one another under identical conditions. The plots would have to be seeded, weeded, fertilized, and watered in exactly the same way, and established in soil of comparable quality and subjected to the same quirks of nature. Ideally the only difference between the plots should be in the "treatment variables," which in this case are the varieties of spinach. If there were any significant difference in yield between plots, we would be justified in drawing the conclusion that the difference was due to the variety of spinach grown. Unlike the scenario presented in *The Spinach Saga*, this would, indeed, be an experiment.

PROBLEM STATEMENT AND HYPOTHESIS

Before carrying out such an experiment, you should have a clear idea of what you want to accomplish. For example:

> I want to know if Green Thunder spinach produces more than Gray Wilt, the variety I have used in the

past, when both are grown under normal conditions in my garden.

The casual observations made during your initial encounters with Green Thunder (when you simply planted it without monitoring its growing conditions) may have led you to believe you had a winner; therefore you hypothesize:

Green Thunder is a better producer than Gray Wilt when grown in my garden.

The hypothesis must be formulated in such a way that it can be either proven or disproven by an experimental test. Notice that the hypothesis does not say that Green Thunder is better than any other variety of spinach, since that could not be proven without comparing it to all spinach— virtually an impossibility. Notice also that you will only measure how well the spinach does when grown in *your* garden, since local growing conditions are very important in determining the success or failure of a crop. These limitations make this a workable hypothesis.

SIMPLE EXPERIMENTS
AND FACTORIAL EXPERIMENTS

Your experiment can either be "simple," testing just one set of variables (in this case, the variety of spinach), or it can be "factorial," testing more than one set of variables simultaneously. Since most biological phenomena are influenced by more than one factor concurrently, a factorial experiment sets up more realistic conditions on which to base conclusions.

If the gardener of our play were to follow his adventure with a controlled experiment, he might wish to know how great an effect all that extra manure and rock phosphate had on the success of his spinach crop. A two-factor experiment, with the different varieties of spinach as one factor and the different levels of manure application as the other, would answer that question. (See Figure 1-1.) If two varieties of spinach were each grown at three levels of manure application, then a total of six plots would be needed, one for each treatment.[2]

A 2-Factor Experiment

simple experiment:
2 plots

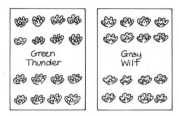

factorial experiment:
2 varieties spinach × 3 levels of manure application =
6 treatments using 6 plots

Figure 1-1

Each treatment represents a different procedure. The purpose of doing a comparative experiment is to find out if it really matters whether one procedure is used rather than another. In the experiment illustrated in Figure 1-1, the six treatments represent all the possible combinations of the two varieties of spinach grown with three different amounts of fertilizer.

The results might show that the spinach yield does not vary with the treatment, or they might show that Green Thunder always produces more spinach, or they might show that Green Thunder has a higher yield than the other variety only when it is heavily manured. It may well be that Green Thunder was bred to be grown only in nitrogen-rich soils and that it does exceedingly well under those conditions, whereas it produces poorly and tastes awful when grown in less nutrient-laden situations. Gray Wilt may never produce as much as Green Thunder does at its best, but it may make a reasonable showing even on less fertile land.

This type of result shows how important it is that a new variety or a new procedure be introduced on a trial basis and in comparison with a method you are accustomed to. Only then, with the standard method as your "control" or point of comparison, can you begin to figure out if the new procedure is to your advantage.

Depending on the cost and availability of fertilizer, one variety or the other may better suit the needs of an individual gardener or farmer. A factorial experiment can pinpoint interactions of cost, yield, nutrient deficiency, variety, etc., which would be overlooked with just a simple experiment. The advantages of a factorial experiment must, however, be weighed against its greater complexity—both in carrying it out and in analyzing it.

RESEARCH THAT IS NOT EXPERIMENTAL

The analyzing of an experiment (which is discussed in Chapter 9) is what makes your work "research" rather than just an exercise. But not all research is experimental: research can also be done in libraries—and living rooms—by reading, synthesizing, and evaluating the experimental work of others. (Working your way through the maze of information available to you is, in fact, the subject of the next chapter.)

Then, too, there is the kind of research I like to call "experimenting with." It is different from "doing an experiment" since it does not set out to prove or disprove hypotheses and usually does not try to compare different options. It is the stage of research which deals with observing and playing around with ideas, for trying out possibilities. Out of this beginning, hypotheses are developed; later, they can be subjected to rigorous testing.

"Experimenting with" is what most of us gardeners are doing when being our most creative: developing new methods and more appropriate tools, struggling with yet another scheme to protect our fruit from the birds and our vegetables from the bugs, trying our hand at plant breeding, or—like the protagonist of The Spinach Saga—planting a new variety.

Yes, "experimenting with" was what he was doing and, encouraged by the results of that first season, the next year he could have gone on and conducted a comparative experiment to see if Green Thunder really was the superior spinach. But he, as many of us would have been tempted to do in the same situation, rushed matters and smudged the distinction between "doing an experiment" and "experimenting with." He went ahead and drew conclusions from an experiment that did not happen. Beware of falling into the same trap as the Spinach Saga-teer. Instead, recognize the intrinsic value of developmental projects as stimuli both for the psyche and for science, and leave the drawing of final conclusions for more formal experimentation.

Just about any formal experiment needs to have been preceded by the "experimenting with" phase. Sometimes you can do that work yourself—you have an idea, begin to develop it, shape it, refine it, draw up a hypothesis, and then carry out an experiment to test that hypothesis. But other times, whether you realize it or not, much of that preparatory work has already been done for you. When you buy seed of two varieties of a vegetable to see which produces better in your garden, your own experiment comes at the end of a long developmental process of breeding and selecting for those seeds.

PARTICIPATING IN RESEARCH

Sometimes this work is best done with the participation of many people. One valuable project that has involved thousands of people and which will probably make a significant impact on the national landscape has been the effort to nudge along the reappearance of the American chestnut tree following the blight which nearly obliterated it earlier this century. In the laboratory, pathologists are working to develop a less virulent strain of the disease fungus and geneticists have been trying to produce a disease-resistant cross between the American and other species of chestnut.[3] Folks all over the eastern half of the country have been tromping through the woods looking for trees that survived the blight and for sprouts from the old root stock which have reached maturity and produced burrs and nuts.[4] They are spurred on by their occasional success and the hope that, against all odds, they can find the chestnut which will produce a disease resistant tree that will repopulate the eastern hardwoods with its offspring.

Nuts and seedlings from the apparently resistant trees are being passed from one individual to the next. Some of the trees from these origins are now reaching the flowering and fruit stages, though it is possible they still may succumb to the blight.[5] The quest for the resistant chestnut tree has captured the imaginations of many dedicated people, fascinated with being a part of this grass-roots research and development effort.

This is not the only ongoing participatory research project. For several years, Rodale Press has been involving readers of *Organic Gardening* magazine in a research project to test the suitability of amaranth as a vegetable and grain for the home gardens of North America. During the summer of 1977 over 10,000 people experimented with growing amaranth!

George (Doc) and Katy Abraham, the well-known gardeners who write "The Green Thumb" column which appears in many local newspapers, have asked readers to experiment with feeding human birth control pills to their plants and to send them reports of their results. It seems some people are finding birth control pills effective as plant stimulants; the Abrahams want to see if this is a consistent response.

The Seed Saver Exchange is a surefire stimulant to planting, if not to the plants themselves. It is an organization that was started in the mid-1970s by Kent Whealy, a plant lover and journalist, to encourage people to save and share the seeds of "heirloom" vegetable varieties. Whealy publishes an annual newsletter with the names of many seed savers and the news of their homegrown research.[6]

And I bet that you can find out about—or start—other research projects through local gardening clubs, food-buying cooperatives, or extension courses. Some research work, like the projects I have just mentioned, need the

(Continued on page 12)

Box 1-1: Ideas for Experimentation

What follows are some of the many questions you can research in your garden. Depending on what *you* want to find out, any one project can be approached and evaluated in many different ways.

Say that your goal is to have ripe tomatoes by the Fourth of July. You could do an experiment in which you prune some of the tomato plants to see if that affects how rapidly the tomatoes ripen. Then on the Fourth of July, you could compare the number of ripe tomatoes on pruned and unpruned plants.

But that is not all you can find out from doing this one experiment. You could also evaluate the quality of fruit—how it looks and how it tastes; you could compare the amount of time and energy that was required to care for each plot; or you could measure the total yield of the plants grown by each of the two methods. It all depends on what information best answers the questions on your mind.

Many of the ideas mentioned here are dealt with in greater detail in the following chapters. We will talk about the way an experiment ought to be set up and how the results can be evaluated so that you can rely on your own research to come up with reasonable solutions to some of your gardening problems.

AREAS TO INVESTIGATE

Compost Creations
Do additives (compost starters, earthworms) make compost better or faster? How big a pile is best? How does aerobic (with oxygen) decomposition compare with anaerobic (without oxygen)?

Working with Weather
Play with planting and harvesting dates, with successional plantings, and with transplantings to stretch the growing season. Manipulate mini-climates to see the effect on plant growth. Watch as insect populations vary with the progress of the season.

(Continued)

Catering to Crops
Should you stake, mulch, irrigate, or prune it? Do your plants thrive on music; does it depend on the melody? (See Retallack 1973; Weinberger and Measures 1968.) What is their response to planting density?

Pressures from Pests
Compare biological, chemical, physical, and mechanical controls. What about introduced parasitoids and predators (the ladybug beetles, praying mantises, Trichogrammatidae wasps)?

Something in the Soil
How do added compost, fertilizers, and minerals affect matters; which nutrient should be added, how much, when, and how (to the top of the soil or dug in below)?

New Crops/New Varieties
Try new varieties and compare their yields. Introduce plants unfamiliar to you and not commonly cultivated in your area.

Putting in Plots
Do roadside gardens suffer from pollutants; would a shrub barrier shield them? Does a garden near a hedgerow or an old field have more or less than its share of pests and beneficial insects? How about birds and other animal life? What effects do exposure (north, south, east, or west) and placement (hilltop, hillside, or bottomland) have on your growing season and success?

Companion Crops

Which combinations are friendly? Why? How close do they like to be? How many of each? Which crop goes in first so that one does not smother the other? How about planting vegetables under fruit trees in an orchard?

Sowing the Seeds

How do new seeds compare with old seeds? What about seeds you have saved yourself vs. those purchased from various seed companies vs. those bred specifically to be grown in an organic garden? Try soaking seeds before sowing, subjecting seeds to magnetic or electrostatic fields, inoculating them, or coating them with clay. Compare germination rates of seeds sown in darkness vs. those sown in the light. Compare seeds sown in different phases of the moon. How does temperature affect germination rate and percentage?

Soils

What about soil preparation? Which works best: plowing deeply (French Intensive) or shallowly, or mulching and then not tilling at all?

DATA TO COLLECT AND EVALUATE

You can evaluate your experimental plots for:

    aesthetics
    yield (total and marketable or top-grade)
    growth rates
    vigor and hardiness
    nutrient value

(Continued)

taste
disease and pest damage
energy requirements
effect on the soil:
    water and nutrient levels
    erodibility
    organisms
    compaction
ecological effects
costs

cooperation of many people. Other projects—such as deciding which variety of spinach grows best in your garden—are things you can do by yourself.

From some of this research you can expect immediate benefits in the form of bigger, better, or entirely new crops. Other research questions may appeal more to your long-range goals and ideals. Soil erosion from your garden may not be something you have thought about before, but once you do, you will realize how important it is to develop methods of cultivation which will prevent your topsoil from blowing or washing away. (For ideas and experiments on this subject, see Chapter 8.) The benefits may or may not be immediately apparent, but they certainly will become evident if you expect to be gardening on the same plot for a while or if you are hoping that your children or grandchildren or others of their generation will be gardening there.

It is not as though crop and soils research is not already being done; it is. But with the exception of efforts of some seed companies and a few others, most of the agricultural research projects of government and industry tend to be for the benefit of large, commercial, mechanized farms. They simply do not suit the needs of gardeners, small-scale farmers, environmentalists, nature buffs, or managers of small woodlots. Our goals are often different; for example:

- The companies that grow lettuce in California [7] and ship it around the country need a lettuce that has been bred for toughness so it can withstand the trip. But when we grow lettuce in our gardens for home use or to sell at a local market, we want lettuce that has been bred for flavor and nutrient quality, not for durability.

- The type of banana now grown in Latin America was chosen because it ripens uniformly so that bunches can be picked green and shipped to distant markets. Likewise, many of the vegetables grown for commercial sale are most profitable when they ripen all at once so that they can be machine-picked. Most of us gardeners, on the other hand, want our produce to ripen a little at a time so we can enjoy our harvest for as long as possible.

- Large, energy-intensive farms rely heavily on chemical pesticides and herbicides, while those of us with gardens in our backyards are not likely to be as willing to introduce these poisons into the air and soil around our homes and into the food we eat. Since World War II, however, the research emphasis has been on chemical pest controls while, in the meantime, investigations into the biological and physical control measures that we would prefer to use have been a low-priority item.

So where do we go to find solutions to our gardening and farming problems? Fortunately there are a few wonderful and inspiring research groups and farm-products businesses that have been looking into the problems and potential of an alternative agriculture for both the small garden and larger farm. But we cannot put the entire burden on these few groups; they do not have the resources to investigate all the areas which concern us.

It is more fun and more rewarding to answer some of the questions ourselves by doing our own experimenting. After all, who is more motivated by *your* pet project than you? With the experience you gain from doing research and experimental work, you will find yourself better able to apply research findings to your own particular needs and . situations. And as the idea of doing research becomes demystified, you will become more capable of analyzing and interpreting the work others do and the advice they give. You will be able to notice their flaws and pick up on their brilliant insights.

The problem is, however, that since most of us have not been trained to do research, our efforts are at times more enthusiastic than accurate. Accuracy can be coupled with enthusiasm, however, if we learn to apply the fundamentals of the scientific method to our garden experimenting.

In this book, we proceed more or less in the order that your research will take, beginning with how to do preparatory research—both the kind that is done by reading and the type done in the field. Then we go on to setting up and carrying out an experiment and conclude with the collection of data and analysis of the results.

Notes

1. A "plot" is the smallest discrete unit in an experiment. Each separate plot is treated differently while within a plot everything is treated equally. We usually think of a plot "of ground," but when the word is used in the technical sense, it can also refer to a group of animals treated in the same manner or to a flat of seedlings in a greenhouse.

2. To actually do this experiment properly, the experiment should be repeated or "replicated" several times. Replicating an experiment is discussed in Chapter 3. If this experiment were replicated three times, it would require 18 plots.

3. The blight was first introduced to the United States at Long Island, New York, in 1904 from eastern Asia. Asiatic species of chestnut (genus *Castanea*), long accustomed to the disease in their midst, had developed a resistance to it not shared by the American and European species. Breeders have attempted to cross these resistant Asiatic varieties with the more statuesque American species.

4. The chestnut tree sends up sprouts from stumps left when old trees are cut down or die. The disease fungus (*Endothia parasitica*) is harbored in the roots, which themselves are not affected by the blight, so almost invariably the sprouts contract the disease and die. Usually this happens before they reach maturity, but occasionally the sprout trees reach the stage of flowering and fruiting. Perhaps the relative longevity of these sprouts indicates a greater resistance to the blight. On this premise people have been collecting the nuts and planting them (the Brooklyn Botanical Gardens coordinated these efforts nearly 40 years ago). Usually the planted trees have no greater resistance than their ancestors, but some of the trees from these origins are attaining maturity. Large mature chestnut trees have been found in the woods throughout the former range of the tree. Nuts from these trees are being planted and the seedlings tended to with great care. For more information on these propagation efforts, see the article by Herman S. Forest in the August 1978 issue of the *Conservationist* entitled "The American Chestnut in New York."

5. And, if a tree lives to maturity, do we immediately proclaim that a disease-resistant strain has been found and that the chestnut is making a comeback? No! We express cautious optimism and then perform a controlled experiment. What this might involve is growing a large number of trees from nuts of that first tree to see how many of these survive. This type of work is going on now.

6. Addresses for these and other groups which encourage participatory research are listed in Appendix II.

7. Some 95 percent of the lettuce sold in the United States is grown on farms in California.

2

Background Information

When a subject first strikes your fancy as an area for investigation, chances are you will have a pretty lopsided idea of what the problem encompasses and practical ways to deal with it. This lopsidedness can, indeed, bring fresh insights and inspiration to a study. But it can also bring the frustration produced by tackling a problem far too big to handle or one with subtleties you had not thought of before.

What you should do is find out as much about the subject as possible before beginning your fieldwork. Start by writing down the research problem and your proposal for dealing with it. Put one copy of the proposal away so that you can look back on it later; it can remind you of what your goals were when you first began.

Keep another copy of the proposal with you to modify as you search for background information on your subject. The search can include talking to experienced people as well as reading the reports of researchers working in your experimental field. You may also want to compile pertinent information on matters such as the soil in your area, the crop you will be working with, the insects you will be monitoring, or the treatment variables you will be testing. Perhaps years of practical experience mean you have this information at your fingertips, but you might have a long winter in which to investigate the matter fully and find out what others have to say.

What follows will introduce those with the time and the inclination to the intricacies of a research library as well as to the research facilities of a public library. The procedures to follow in making a complete search for information on any subject are explained in detail.

Now if you don't want to deal with all these possible avenues of search, you can get a start by looking up your subject in one of the encyclopedias you see on the library shelf or get the name of a book from one of those suggested in this or other bibliographies. If you are already quite familiar with the subject area, look up your topic in the most appropriate of the indexes listed under Step 6 later in this chapter, find several pertinent articles, and use the references in them to further your search. Even if it is just a quick bit of data you are after, the source books recommended later should be helpful in speeding your search.

STEP 1: RESEARCH LOG

You will avoid much befuddlement as well as retracing of steps by keeping a record of what you are doing in a research log. Put your original research proposal in a conspicuous place to keep you centered. Record the sources you consult and the "key words" you look under in each of them. Make note of resource people you talk with and the questions you ask.

I find it helpful to use a card file with 3 x 5-inch index cards (see Figure 2-1). I use a separate index card for any book or article I intend to read. Once I have looked at the reference, I write down a brief note on the pertinent information I found in it. I also keep a few pages of the log

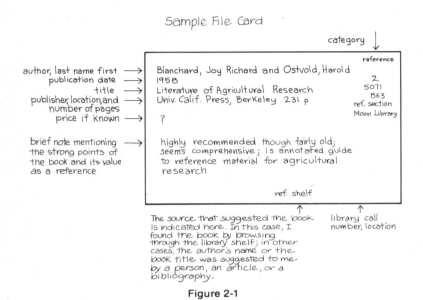

Sample File Card

Figure 2-1

reserved for a running list of things to do and leads to pursue, crossing things off as they are done and adding new things as they occur to me.

STEP 2: THE LIBRARY

Taking some time to find out about a library's facilities is worthwhile. It is important to know whom the library proposes to serve. Is it a public library or is it designed as an academic research facility? Ask the librarian for help in defining the scope of the library's holdings, especially insofar as specialty areas or "holes" occur in the collection. It can be misleading to work exclusively with the material in a library not suited to your needs. After all, you might be led to believe that your subject, say "plant breeding," has had no work done in it for 50 years.

Do not delude yourself, however, as to your needs. If you are just beginning, a basic book or readily available government document—such as one of the Yearbooks of Agriculture—may be all you need to get you started.

But if you do need a specialized library, there are several directories (Young, Young, and Kruzas 1977) which list libraries by geographic area and subject strengths as well as telling whether the facilities are open to the public. Perhaps the best libraries for gardening or agricultural research are those of the public agricultural colleges.

STEP 3: DEFINING YOUR TOPIC AND USING REFERENCE BOOKS

Once you have a fairly good sense of the facility you are working in, you can begin researching your topic. Start by reading a summary or review article to get an idea of the breadth of the field and its interrelated parts. The article will, perhaps, suggest a manageable project for your fieldwork.

There are several paths you can follow to find such an article. Using reference books to find additional material is discussed here (also see Step 4, below). To locate a general reference book, look in the subject card catalog under:

Reference Books—Bibliography

or

Bibliography—Bibliography

These listings may turn up such material as Sheehy's *Guide to Reference Books* or Walford's *Guide to Reference Material*. Both of these are subdivided by subject area and suggest more specific reference material in the field of agriculture or whatever.

General reference books give you a broad idea of what has been published, but to know what is available in your own library, look in the subject card catalog under:

"Subject"—Bibliography

e.g.: **Agriculture—Bibliography**

or

Biology—Bibliography

Do not use more specific search terms at this point because you will bypass valuable reference guides.

Under **Agriculture—Bibliography** you will be referred to material like Smith and Reid's *Guide to the Literature of the Life Sciences* or Grogan's *Science and Technology: an Introduction to the Literature* or Blanchard and Ostvold's *Literature of Agricultural Research*. These books can be *very* helpful in directing your search.

But at this point you are still trying to find an appropriate summary article. From one of the reference guides, get the names of several general or subject encyclopedias. If you have not located a reference guide, look in the subject card catalog under:

Encyclopedias and Dictionaries

or, for more specialized sources, under:

"Subject"—Dictionaries
e.g.: **Science—Dictionaries**
or
Agriculture—Dictionaries
or
Gardening—Dictionaries

The "dictionary" listing includes word-finding books as well as compilations of longer articles which we generally think of as encyclopedias.

Annual reviews, which are published in many subject areas, are another source of review articles. These tend to be quite academic with many references to primary research work. The reference guides mention some of these review journals or you can look in the subject card catalog under:

"Subject"—Collected Works
e.g.: **Agriculture—Collected Works**

Some of the agriculturally oriented review journals (the year indicates the first year of publication) are:

Advances in Agronomy, Academic Press, 1949

Advances in Botanical Research, Academic Press, 1963

Advances in Ecological Research, Academic Press, 1962

Advances in Food Research, Academic Press, 1948

Agricultural Science Review, Cooperative State Research Service, USDA, 1963

Annual Review of Entomology, Annual Reviews, 1956

Botanical Review, New York Botanical Gardens, 1935

World Review of Pest Control, Fision Pest Control, Cambridge, England, 1962

Neither the guides to reference literature nor the subject card catalog listings tell you what *specific* articles are to be found in the review volumes. For this you must go to the book itself and look in the index. Another possibility is to use the *Index to Scientific Reviews*, a computerized index begun in 1974, probably available only in research libraries.

Reader's Guide to Periodical Literature, on the other hand, is a review index that is almost universally available. Unlike the more academic indexes (see Step 6 below), *Reader's Guide* covers articles from popular magazines which are available in many public libraries.

STEP 4: LOOKING FOR BOOKS— USING THE CARD CATALOG

If you used a reference guide, you now should have names of books, encyclopedias, or review journals you would like to find on the shelves. Or perhaps you already know the titles of some pertinent books. To find out which of these your library has and where they are located, use the author/title card catalog.

If you do not have the name of a specific book, but want to see what the library has in a certain subject area, use the subject card catalog. In some libraries the catalogs are combined into one "dictionary" catalog. Most academic libraries use subject headings (or "search words") determined by the Library of Congress. These are listed in a reference book called, appropriately, *Library of Congress Subject Headings*. It is helpful to use this book first to decide which search words to use before looking in the card catalog.

Terms used by the Library of Congress are printed in bold letters. Terms not used as Library of Congress subject headings may be listed followed by "see . . . ," directing you to a related heading that is used. Each subject heading has a "call number" which identifies all books on that subject. The call number is given in parentheses following the headings, e.g., **Plant breeding** (SB123). Since books are generally arranged by subject, the call number also tells you where in the library your book is located. Thus, by looking under the appropriate subject heading, you have the option to bypass the card catalog and go directly to the shelves of books to see what is available. Of course, this means you will miss anything currently in circulation.

It is also possible that your search words are too general; you could waste a lot of time leafing through cards to find something useful. If, for instance, you looked in the card catalog under "Breeding," having in mind to do an experiment on plant breeding, you might turn up instead a book on etiquette by Emily Post. By first using the book of subject headings, you would find **Breeding** followed by *sa*, meaning "see also," directing you to a number of more specific terms, including **Plant breeding.**

With your carefully chosen list of search words, you can now leaf through the cards in the card catalog to find out which books your library in fact possesses. These small cards contain a great deal of information. In particular, note the numbered words or phrases on the bottom of the card. These are called "tracings" and list all the headings in the catalog under which the book is filed. They tell you about different facets of the book's subject matter and add to your list of potential search words.

Also note the "call number," usually printed in the upper left corner of the card. It represents both the subject classification of the book and its location in the library. There are several classification systems in use.

The Dewey Decimal System, used in many public libraries, is based on Francis Bacon's "Chart of Human Learning." Its ten major subject classes are each represented by a single integer:

0—general (including reference)
1—philosophy and psychology
2—religion
3—social sciences
4—languages
5—pure sciences
6—applied sciences
7—arts
8—literature
9—geography and history

Each major class is divided into ten subclasses; 630–639 are set aside for "agriculture and agricultural industries."

630—general works
631—farming activities
632—plant diseases and pests and control
633—production of field crops
634—orchards, fruits, and forestry
635—garden crops (horticulture)
636—animal husbandry
637—dairy
638—insect culture
639—nondomesticated animals and plants

The "nonapplied" aspects of the biological world are indexed with the pure sciences in the 500s.

570–579—life sciences (574—biology)
580–589—botanical sciences
590–599—zoological sciences

Further subdivisions of knowledge are conveyed with numbers after the decimal. This linear system has become quite cumbersome with the great explosion of written information of the last half-century. Also, since all the numbers were assigned when the system was first developed, there is no room for new fields of knowledge, a shortcoming particularly felt in scientific and technological fields.

The Library of Congress System, with its use of both letters and numbers on several lines, can classify a tremendous amount of information and is, therefore, used in most research libraries. The "class number" on the first line refers to subject matter. The first letter is the most general level of classification, made more specific by the second letter and then by the numbers which follow. All works on precisely the same subject have the same class number, which is also the case in any library using the Library of Congress System. Some of the combinations an agricultural researcher might use are:

H—social science
  HC79—environmental policy
Q—science
  QC—physics (including climatological data)
  QH—natural history
  QH301–705—biology
  QH540—ecology
  QH545—environmental effects on plants and animals
  QK—botany
  QK746–759—plants
  QL—zoology

S—agriculture
    SB—horticulture and plant culture
    SD—forestry
    SF—animal culture
    SH—fish culture
    SK—hunting sports

T—technology
    TR—photography

Z—bibliography

Below the class number is the "book number," by which each book in a library is kept distinct from all others. It consists of a letter, usually the first initial of the author's last name, followed by a number. The unit is treated as a decimal number whether or not a decimal point is printed. Thus A143 is shelved before A9.

The call number might also include a subdivision of the class number, a volume or copy number, or the date of publication. A location symbol is used if the book is kept somewhere different than the call number itself would indicate, such as in the archives or in the reference room.

The spine of the book *Hunger Signs in Crops* is illustrated in Figure 2-2, starting with the title and the mention that it is the third edition of the book. Following that is the last name of the editor of this edition. At the very bottom is the name of the publisher. The five lines in between make up the call number. "SB" is the classification for "horticulture and plant culture," a division of "agriculture" (which has the symbol "S"). The "742" is a further subdivision; these two lines together make up the class number. The rest of the information comprises the book number, which can differ from library to library. "H" is the initial of the editor of the *first* edition, since it was at that time that the book was first cataloged. This edition was published in 1964 and the library from which the book was borrowed has at least two copies.

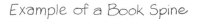

Example of a Book Spine

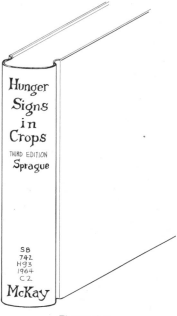

Hunger
Signs
in
Crops
THIRD EDITION
Sprague

SB
742
H93
1964
C 2
McKay

Figure 2-2

STEP 5: LOOKING ELSEWHERE FOR BOOKS

Not all the books you need will be available in your library. If you are interested in purchasing a book, you might look to see if it is in the latest annual edition of *Books in Print*, a multivolume listing of books currently available (thereby considered to be "in print") from most United States publishers. Libraries and bookstores will likely have a copy of *Books in Print* because it is regularly used for book ordering. If your book is listed, you can special order it through a local bookstore. The *Cumulative Book Index* serves a similar function on an international scale for books published in English.

A third option is to make use of Interlibrary Loan, a

system which enables patrons of one library to use books and periodicals belonging to another library.

Finally you could use a library directory, as mentioned earlier, to find out about other facilities in your region which would be likely to carry the type of material you are looking for. These directories are listed in the subject card catalog under:

Libraries—Directories

or

Libraries, Special—U.S.—Directories

STEP 6: INDEXES AND ABSTRACTS

When, as a biology student, I received my first research assignment, it was on the breeding habits of *Scolytus multistriatus*, the species of beetle responsible for carrying the Dutch elm disease. Blithely I went to the subject card catalog and looked up "beetles," finding, much to my dismay, just a few references to taxonomic keys. I was shocked at the poverty of this library which specialized in forestry yet had pitifully little information on one of the major entomological problems of the day.

Shortly thereafter, in embarrassed relief, I discovered the key to the vastness of library resources. It resides in magazines and journals! Much of the information in research libraries is not in book form at all, but in the much more frequently published and, therefore, more up-to-date periodicals. If your interest in research maintains sufficient momentum, you may eventually want to seek out these sources of primary information.

Although you may subscribe to one or a few magazines in your area of interest, you would have neither the time to read nor, probably, the finances to afford all the journals whose articles touch on your subject area. The number of publications is overwhelming. Sorting out this constant spew of information is a major challenge.

Many libraries and individual researchers receive a

weekly pamphlet called *Current Contents* which reproduces the tables of contents of a number of journals. The
reader can rapidly see what is being discussed in his or her
broad area of interest. *Current Contents* is published in
several series, the one most applicable for our purposes
being *Agriculture, Biology and Environmental Science.*

If, on the other hand, you want material on a given
subject published over an extended period of time, indexing
and abstracting services will help you. They work in much
the same way as the index of a book, but instead of catego-
rizing material from just one publication, the articles from
many periodicals are classified together. Many of these indexes go a step further than just listing citations, including
a summary paragraph called an "abstract." This can be in-
credibly valuable, particularly if much of the material you
are looking for is in a foreign language or is otherwise difficult to find.

As mentioned previously, if you are working in a public
library, *Reader's Guide to Periodical Literature* may be the
only index available to you. It covers general-interest publications with articles of varying scope and depth, a number
of which would no doubt be quite useful. If, however, you
want to see reports of original research, you will probably
need to use the indexes of a research library.

Each of the indexes in the following list covers some
aspect of the agricultural sciences. While they overlap in
some of the journals they include, each has a different emphasis. It would be rare for a library to have all or most of
these indexes. Nevertheless try to find the index best suited
to your needs since it can be quite time-consuming to do a
literature search through more than one or two indexes.

Selected Indexes for Use in Agricultural Research

Abstracts of Entomology: taken from the more
general *Biological Abstracts* and *BioResearch
Index*

Abstracts of Mycology: from *Biological Abstracts*
and *BioResearch Index*

Agricultural and Horticultural Engineering

Agrindex: published by FAO Rome, citations only; international

Agronomy Abstracts: papers presented at annual meetings of American Society of Agronomy, Crop Science Society, and the Soil Science Society of America

Bibliography of Agriculture: National Agricultural Library holdings

Bibliography of Soil Science, Fertilizers and General Agronomy

Biography Index: covers 1,900 nonbiographical publications; lists by name and by profession

Biological Abstracts: covers 8,129 serials; part of BIOSIS computer base

Biological and Agricultural Index: superseded *Agricultural Index*

BioResearch Index: covers symposia, review journals, translated journals, institute reports; part of BIOSIS computer base

Commercial Fisheries Abstracts

Current Contents: reproduces tables of contents from many journals

Directory of Published Proceedings (INTERDOK)-Series SEMP: bibliographic directory of preprints and published proceedings of conventions and meetings

Dissertation Abstracts: abstracts of doctoral dissertations submitted to University Microfilms by more than 345 cooperating schools in the United States and Canada

Entomology Abstracts: covers more than 4,300 serials

Experiment Station Record: 95 volumes, from 1886 to 1946, abstracting work at each of the experiment stations

FAO Documentation—Current Bibliography and Current Index: holdings of the Food and Agricultural Organization of the United Nations

Fertilizer Abstracts: fertilizer marketing,
technology

Field Crop Abstracts: published in Great Britain

Food Science and Technology: international

Forestry Abstracts

Government Reports Announcement and Index:
government-sponsored research and development
reports available from NTIS

Herbage Abstracts: grasslands, pasture plants, and
fodder crops

Horticultural Abstracts: British

Index to Scientific Reviews: index of review and
summary articles

Masters Abstracts: abstracts of theses available on
University Microfilms

Meteorological and Geoastrophysical Abstracts:
world literature in environmental sciences,
meteorology, astrophysics, hydrosphere
hydrology, glaciology, and oceanography

*Monthly Catalogue of U.S. Government
Publications:* material available from the
Superintendent of Documents

Nutrition Abstracts and Reviews: chemical
composition of foods and vitamins, physiology

Plant Breeding Abstracts: plant breeding and
genetics

Review of Applied Entomology: part A—economic
entomology; part B—medical and veterinary
entomology

Review of Plant Pathology

Science Citation Index: covers 2,700 serials;
researcher looks up name of known author and is
referred to newer articles which cite that author
in bibliography

Soils and Fertilizers: soil classification, crop
production, plant protection, agricultural systems;
international

Sports Fishery Abstracts: limnology, ecology,
  natural history

Weed Abstracts: weeds and weed control;
  international

Zoological Record: systematic zoology

STEP 7: USING PERIODICALS

Periodicals are issued periodically; that's what differentiates them from books. They include publications issued on a regular basis—the type most of us know simply as "magazines," as well as more research-oriented publications called journals. Some periodicals appear too sporadically to be considered journals and are called "serials," meaning anything appearing in successive parts. And to confuse matters, the word "serials" is sometimes used to refer to *all* periodicals.

Serials are identified by volume, usually with a new one each year, and by number if more than one issue is put out for a volume. Usually the page numbers of the second issue continue where the first left off, so that February's journal may begin with page 132. A reference in an index or bibliography to *"Science* 3(4):156–172" means volume 3, number 4, pages 156 to 172.

To find an article, first see if your library carries the serial it is in. If it does not, you may be able to request a copy of the article via Interlibrary Loan. There are several reference books which help you locate libraries carrying certain periodicals, such as *Chemical Abstracts Service Source Index* and *Union List of Serials in the United States and Canada.* You could also write to the author requesting a reprint copy.

STEP 8: GOVERNMENT DOCUMENTS

Some of the best compilations of information are published by the federal government. The Department of Agriculture's Yearbooks of Agriculture and its Agricultural

Handbooks are particularly useful. You will be lucky, however, if you have a lead on valuable government publications, because searching through the mass of government listings can be like looking for the proverbial needle in the haystack. Your county cooperative extension agents can often direct you to the most useful information.

Even if you know what you are looking for, you may have trouble finding it. Some libraries mix government publications with other material; others catalog and store it separately. Material is often filed under the corporate author, which is the name of the government agency, rather than under the name of the individual who wrote it. If you are having trouble finding something or even finding out what is available, speak to a librarian. They seem universally sympathetic to people trying to deal with the maze of governmental information.

Many of the more popular publications of the various government departments are sold to the public by the Government Printing Office, which now handles nearly 25,000 titles. New titles and revisions are listed in the *Monthly Catalogue of U.S. Government Publications*.

Some 1,200 federal depository libraries throughout the country receive a copy of all this material. Reference books which list depository libraries are in the subject card catalog under:

Libraries—Depository

There are also 25 federal bookstores which sell the most popular government publications. A list of these stores is available from the Superintendent of Documents, from whom you can also order a free *Subject Bibliography Index* (SB–999) listing 270 subject bibliographies. Write: Superintendent of Documents, U.S. Government Printing Office, Washington, D.C. 20402.

Your congressperson receives 200 complimentary copies of each Yearbook of Agriculture to distribute to constituents and is authorized by law to provide, free of charge, other Department of Agriculture and Department of Health, Education and Welfare material in limited quantity.

Federally sponsored research and development reports and other technical analyses prepared by government agencies or by private research groups on contract with the government are indexed in *Government Reports Announcement and Index*. These materials are sold by the National Technical Information Service (NTIS), 5285 Port Royal Road, Springfield, Virginia 22161. These publications are not automatically sent to depository libraries.

The *Bibliography of Agriculture* indexes all material contained in the National Agricultural Library, both government and nongovernment publications including much foreign material. This bibliography should be available in libraries specializing in agriculture or biology.

Topographic maps are available from the U.S. Geological Survey:

Eastern Office:

U.S. Geological Survey
Branch of Distribution
1200 South Eads Street
Arlington, Virginia 22202

Western Office:

U.S. Geological Survey
Denver Branch of Distribution
Box 25046 Federal Center
Denver, Colorado 80225

Publication of the Geological Survey (Library of Congress call number Z 6034) lists that agency's material.

State cooperative extension service publications also should not be overlooked.

STEP 9: PERSONAL CONTACTS

The people who write scientific articles and do research are real, albeit perhaps very busy, human beings. So while you should not abuse the ability to get in touch with them directly by doing so indiscriminately, it can prove very helpful to be able to contact specialists in various fields.

If, for example, you are observing a certain insect-plant interaction, it is important that you know the species you are working with. Unless your insect is a highly publicized garden pest, it is unlikely that you could make this identification yourself. In such cases it would be nice to be able to find an entomologist to help you.

First, contact your county's cooperative extension service to see if your county agent can recommend a local expert to make the identification. If that fails, look in the subject card catalog in the library under:

"Subject"—Directories

or

"Subject"—Biographies

The Naturalists' Directory, American Men and Women of Science, and several other compilations of names and addresses may be found under:

Science—Directory

Articles in journals and periodicals often give the author's name and address in a footnote on the first page. This enables interested readers to correspond with the author, perhaps to get copies of other articles he or she has written, to make a critical comment or to ask a question about the way the experiment was conducted or evaluated.

STEP 10: EVALUATING THE INFORMATION YOU HAVE COLLECTED

Once you have followed through all the preceding steps, you may well have amassed an incredible body of information. The question now is how to use it to help you carry out your own experiment. Most important is that you read all the material with a critical eye.

You may find that some of the information you read appears to be contradictory. That is because you rarely find reports of two or more experiments carried out in exactly the same way, and conclusions which are valid under one set of circumstances do not necessarily apply to experiments carried out under different conditions.

When you read secondary sources (which are the reviews, the encyclopedias, and the public interest books), you must be careful that neither you nor the author of the summary article attributes more to the original data than is legitimate. Be careful when extrapolating results from one set of experimental conditions to other situations.

With experience in reading reports of original research, you will get a sense of the limitations which experimental conditions impose on broad conclusions. This will help you in evaluating any reports you read and will help you in deciding what information found in other reports can be applied to your own research. Research papers are usually prepared using the following format: introduction, literature review, materials and methods, results and discussion, and conclusion. These may be discretely labeled sections or may flow together. Some journals also require the author to prepare an abstract. Knowing what to expect in each of these sections will make your interpretation of the report more meaningful.

An *abstract* or *synopsis* is either at the very beginning or very end of a paper, often printed in smaller type than the rest and is usually the part reprinted by the abstracting services. It outlines the focus of the research and contains the key information without any of the detail.

A brief *introduction* generally leads into a *literature review* of earlier work. If the current research is based on the ideas or methods of previous workers, even to contradict them, a discussion of this earlier research is included. Literature reviews can be very useful for someone trying to get an overview of a new subject area.

The *materials and methods* section deals with the experimental design. Here you may pick up suggestions on technique: how to construct a piece of equipment or when it is best to make an observation. If the experiment is very similar to the one you are planning, you might want to parallel the design precisely so that you can make valid comparisons of the results.

This is also the section that can be gravely disappointing after the excitement of a promising title and introduction. Here you will find out if the research on "energetics in the garden" required the purchase of a $10,000 respirometer. Here you will also find out if the work was done in the field, in a greenhouse or laboratory, or by simulation model on a computer. While each is a valuable research site, the applicability to your project differs.

From the information given in the materials and methods section, you should try to determine if you can trust the experimental design and, hence, the results. Does the data collected answer the question which was originally posed?

Results and discussion is the most freewheeling section of the paper. Each worker can determine how to analyze, graph, and depict the results. You, as the alert reader, should note which data are stressed and which, if any, were omitted. Determine if this affects the interpretation of the results.

The *conclusion* should include only deductions from the data presented with the results. The conclusions you draw may well differ from those of the author and, if that is the case, you should determine why.

Having pulled together a good bit of information to give your experiment an analytical framework, you now are ready to begin thinking about setting up your fieldwork.

For more on information resources and the use of libraries, see Bonn 1973, Bottle 1972, Gates 1973, Lasworth 1972, Morris and Elkins 1978, Schmeckebier and Eastin 1969, and the *Union List of Serials in the Libraries of the United States and Canada*, in addition to those publications already referred to within this chapter.

3

Planning for Your Experiments

This chapter is about setting up a valid experiment in the field, taking into consideration the uncontrollable variables unique to agricultural experimentation—the unpredictability of the weather, the genetics of individual plants, and the differences in soil quality.

First we will discuss each of these variables, then show how different types of plot layouts are used to overcome any problems caused by them. Several projects and tests are suggested to help you better understand your soil and climate so you can make a wiser choice of plot layout for your site and for the type of experiment you are planning. The projects also give you a better sense of the ecology of your garden and, in that light, could be carried out just for fun. If you are anxious to get right on with your experiments, rest assured that doing all of these tests is hardly a prerequisite. With that in mind, let's talk about the weather.

WEATHER

The effects of dry vs. wet conditions, and cold vs. hot summers, are best dealt with by running an experiment for several seasons. Otherwise, the conclusions you draw as to the advantages of one treatment over another are limited by the particular conditions under which your experiment was run. It is of limited value to know only that your snap beans and beets did well together in the summer of 1978 when there was above average rainfall and temperatures were lower than usual since, barring the prophecies of the *Farmer's Almanac*, you have no way of knowing what the growing season will be like when you make your agricultural decisions for the following year.

In any case, weather is a compendium of far greater complexity than several years' worth of temperature and precipitation data alone would indicate. Plant development also depends on the length of the daylight period (the photoperiod), air pressure, wind velocity and frequency of high winds, intensity of rainfall, amount of humidity and dew, snow cover, and length of frost-free period. In addition, insect pestiness and disease cycles fluctuate both dependently and independently of weather conditions. Rather than attempting to analyze the effects of all of these variables on the results of your experiment, you can simply repeat the experiment for several years to see if weather variations affect treatment performance. You can draw tentative conclusions after one season's work if treatment results differ by a great deal.

Another reason for continuing experiments over several years is that it often takes that long before the effects of the different treatments are felt. This would be the case if you were comparing the impact of organic vs. chemical fertilizers on the soil structure, nutrient level, and insect community, or if you were trying different soil tillage methods to see how they affected the rate of erosion.

In addition to climatic variation from year to year, you must be aware of changes as the growing season passes: the photoperiod gets shorter with summer's progress, there are rainy and droughty periods, insects reach different phases

Box 3-1: Making a Rain Gauge

This rain gauge works by collecting precipitation falling over a large area into a narrow vessel so that it is deep enough to take an accurate reading. (Multiply fractions of an inch or millimeters by the ratio between the diameter of the larger surface and the smaller to create a scale for marking the collection tube.) Readings should be taken soon after the rain falls so that water evaporation does not change your measurements.

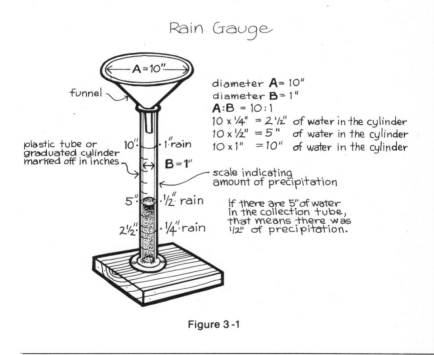

Rain Gauge

funnel

A=10″

plastic tube or
graduated cylinder
marked off in inches

10″ ·1″rain

B=1″

5″ ·½″ rain

2½″ ·¼″·rain

diameter **A**= 10″
diameter **B**= 1″
A:B = 10:1
10 x ¼″ = 2½″ of water in the cylinder
10 x ½″ = 5″ of water in the cylinder
10 x 1″ = 10″ of water in the cylinder

scale indicating
amount of precipitation

If there are 5″of water
in the collection tube,
that means there was
½″ of precipitation.

Figure 3-1

in their life cycles, and competition from other plants varies as their growth peaks and then slows down. Thus, if I did an experiment to find the variety of Swiss chard most "resistant" to spinach leaf miner attack, my results would differ depending on planting date, since the larvae of *Pegomyia hyoscyami*, the spinach leaf miner, seem to thrive in my garden only in spring and early summer.

Your experimental results will serve you better if you keep a record of planting dates and other dates of importance (such as emergence from the soil, flowering, and fruiting) as well as weather data. Maximum-minimum thermometers and rain gauges may be available at your local garden/farm supplier or hardware store, or they can be purchased through one of the biological or gadgetry suppliers listed in Appendix I. Another option is to make your own rain gauge (see Box 3-1).

Collecting weather data yourself is the most accurate method of keeping a record of conditions in your garden. Being your own weatherman, however, requires diligent checking of the rain gauge, thermometer, and other weather-monitoring equipment you may be using. Rather than going to all that trouble, you may prefer to use the *Climatological Data of the United States Weather Bureau*—a series of separate booklets published monthly for each state which provides temperature and precipitation data from each of the national weather stations within the state.

Summaries are compiled after each ten-year period so you can see how weather conditions of the current season compare with the norm for the area from the previous years. Be sure to use data from the weather station nearest to you, or the one with weather conditions most similar to your own.

Climatological Data of the United States Weather Bureau may be available in your library or you can order it from the National Climatic Center, Federal Building, Asheville, North Carolina 28801, Att.: Publications. The cost is $5.10 per year (which includes an annual summary, available separately for $.30), or $.40 for one monthly report. Checks should be made out to the Department of Commerce, NOAA.

The same department publishes *Daily Weather Maps, Weekly Series*, which shows daily weather maps of the entire country. These are available from the Superintendent of

Documents at a yearly subscription rate of $16.50, or $.35 for an individual copy (order number: DWMW–File Code 2E C 55.213).

PLANT INDIVIDUALITY

Due to variation among individual plants, similar to what we take for granted in human beings and dogs, you must take care that each experimental plot is large enough to include a representative sampling that covers the range of the plant's genetic possibilities. Cross-pollinated crops like rye or corn have greater variability than self-pollinated crops like wheat, beans, and barley. Individual characteristics become more important in larger plants— reaching an extreme with trees—since there are fewer plants per given area.

As a further means of keeping tabs on plant variability, you should be certain that you are using seed of equal quality in each treatment plot. Fresh seed of one variety tested against four-year-old seed of another tells more about how well the seed was stored than it does about the relative merits of the two varieties.

SOIL QUALITY

The third uncontrollable variable in agricultural work is the soil. Attempts to compensate for soil heterogeneity are actually the reason the field of experimental design developed. Much of what is now accepted in all the sciences with regard to the design of experiments and statistical technique was devised earlier this century by R. A. Fisher at the Rothamsted Agricultural Experiment Station in England in order to be able to perform valid agricultural experiments.

The soils beneath our feet have been formed by the weathering of rock minerals together with the dead remains and living influence of plants and animals. Soil types differ depending on how long the process has been going on in a particular area, what minerals form the bedrock, the topography, and the climate. Soil types can be identified and have been named and classified. In areas not recently used for agriculture, a trained soil scientist can tell differences in soil quality simply by looking at the lay of the land. However, on agricultural land different crops take nutrients from the soil at varying rates, and fertilizers, especially when applied in strips by agricultural machinery, give the nutrient status of the soil a checkerboard pattern. So, to set up an experiment that avoids a built-in bias due to differences in soil quality, you must really know your soil—both its natural classification and its agricultural history.

Soil Conservation Service Maps

The Soil Conservation Service (SCS) of the U.S. Department of Agriculture (USDA) has published maps and soil evaluations for about half the counties in the country. These are a joint effort of the SCS and various state agencies, usually the agricultural experiment stations, and can be purchased from your county SCS.

The capabilities of area soils are discussed in terms useful for farmers, foresters, engineers, and housebuilders. The maps are large enough to be helpful to users of even small rural holdings, as you can pick out one field from another and even see the hedgerows in between. However, these maps are not suited for urban and suburban gardens where soil has been excavated or imported by building contractors.

Soil Tests—Taking a Soil Sample

You can find out still more about your land by taking a soil sample and testing it for nutrient availability, pH, texture, and water-holding capacity. Since so much hinges on how your small sample performs on the tests, great care must be taken in choosing that sample.

It is wise to test your soil before going on with other research. The tests will pinpoint nutrient deficiencies and also will help you to figure out if there are differences in the quality of the land which you intend to use for your experiment.

If your experimental area is small and you are relatively certain that the soil is homogeneous, then you need to take only one sample. If, however, you want to find out how the soil quality varies, then divide the area into several sections and take a sample from each. If there are obvious differences in the lay of the land, divide it into sections according to topography.

The results from these tests will help you in deciding how to lay out the experimental plots so that no one treatment has an advantage over the others because it is planted on better soil. Plot layouts are discussed later in this chapter.

Each soil sample is made up of at least five soil borings. Each boring is considered one sampling unit. Use a garden trowel to collect the sampling units, each unit being about as much soil as can fit on the trowel. Place the soil from each sample on a large sheet of wrapping paper, such as a grocery bag, and mix it together well. Use your trowel to collect enough soil from this pile to fill a clean quart container.

Samples of agricultural soil are usually taken from the top ten inches or "plow layer," but there is good reason for you to look at the lower layers as well. The characteristics of the subsoil layers or "horizons" contribute to the quality of plant growth. Think about it—after the very beginning of the growing season, how deep are the plant roots? Are they not getting their nutrients and moisture from levels far deeper than the plow layer? Soil classification, in fact, is based in large part on the relationship between the topsoil and the subsoil horizons. Thus, you may learn a great deal by taking samples from different depths. If you do, just make sure samples from the different soil layers are not mixed together but are labeled and analyzed separately.

Soil Nutrient and pH Testing

Soil nutrient testing, also called rapid chemical analysis, works by using chemical extractants known to be able to measure available forms of a nutrient. You can buy a soil test kit from your local farm supply store complete with pH paper and bottles of chemical reactants for testing the major nutrients—nitrogen, phosphorus, and potassium. The instructions for using these kits are quite simple, but the results may not be as precise as you would like. More accurate testing can be arranged through your county cooperative extension office for a nominal fee. They need a cup-size (½ pint) sample for their tests.

You should recognize that the relationship between the nutrients in the soil and the nutrients utilized by plants is complex.[1] Part of the problem is that deficiency or abundance of the big-three nutrients does not tell the whole story of the quality of soil and plants. Micronutrients are also vitally important. Some private chemistry laboratories can test your soil for a wide range of elements. Check the Yellow Pages of your telephone directory under "Chemists—Analytical and Consulting" for listings of local laboratories.

Soil Texture

In addition to a chemical analysis you can do various mechanical analyses of soil components. Soil texture, which is the relative proportion of mineral particles of various sizes, can be determined by a sedimentation study or by the "feel" test. In the human scale of time, texture can be considered a permanent feature of the soil. It is unaltered by cultivation. Texture is basically what determines the proportion of air in the soil, the amount of water and nutrients which are retained or drained away, and the ease with which plant roots penetrate the soil. Almost all soils are a mixture of different particle sizes, each of which is important to a healthy soil.

Sand particles are the largest. Their size, together with their irregular surface, means that they pack together in a bulky way leaving large pockets in between for air and water penetration. Air is needed by plant roots for oxygen, but the water in a sandy soil drains too rapidly by the pull of gravity to be useful to the plants (just think about how fast the sand on a beach dries when the tide goes out). In addition, important soil nutrients are leached away with the draining water.

(Continued on page 50)

Box 3-2: Soil Particle Size Classes (USDA Classification)

Class	Diameter Limits (in mm.)	
stones	>254 (or 10 inches)	
cobbles	76-254 (or 3-10 inches)	
gravel	2-76 (or 2 mm.-3 inches)	
very coarse sand	2.00-1.00	
coarse sand	1.00-0.50	
medium sand	0.50-0.25	
fine sand	0.25-0.10	fine earth
very fine sand	0.10-0.05	
silt	0.05-0.002	
clay	<0.002	

Note: The symbol ">" means "greater than," as in "stones are greater than 254 millimeters."
The symbol "<" means "less than," as in "clay is less than 0.002 millimeters."

Box 3-3: Sedimentation Test

The texture of your garden soil can be evaluated by a do-it-yourself sedimentation test based on the idea that heavier, larger particles settle out of a water suspension faster. "Sand," "silt," and "clay" are the three major size categories of mineral particles in the soil. Since it is known how long it takes for each type of particle to settle, we can measure the depth of the settled soil at the prescribed times, and in this way

(Continued)

45

find how much of our soil is sand, silt, or clay. The relative proportion of these particles is what determines soil texture.

Have ready about a cup of air-dried soil for your sample. Using a kitchen strainer,* sieve out gravel, stones, and organic debris. Crush clumps of particles so they all go through the strainer. Estimate the proportion of gravel and stones. The sieved soil is called "fine earth."

Mix up a solution of Calgon water softener, using 1 tablespoon Calgon† to 1 cup water. The Calgon helps to separate and disperse the individual particles.

For your sedimentation tank you need a jar of at least quart capacity with straight sides (especially at the bottom) and a tight lid. Some wide-mouth canning jars fit the bill as do the jars of some brands of peanut butter. If all you have are jars with curved bottom edges, pour an inch of melted wax into the jar to give it a raised bottom.

Put ½ cup of the soil, several tablespoons of the Calgon solution, and 3 cups of water into the jar and shake it vigorously. If you can spare your food blender for a day or so, you could mix up your concoction in it. Since the blender is wider than most jars, you should use a larger sample (about 1 cup of sieved soil) so the soil separates will be deep enough to measure.

Using a millimeter ruler, take a measurement of the soil which has settled 40 seconds after you stop shaking the jar to get the depth of sand, after 30 minutes to get the depth of silt, and after 12 hours to get the depth of clay and the total reading. If you ever wondered how pottery clay was purified of other soil particles, this test (see Figure 3-2) will answer your question.

(Continued)

* Most kitchen strainers very conveniently have holes close to 2 mm. in diameter, which is the upper size limit of fine earth. Use a millimeter ruler to make sure that the holes in your strainer are the right size.

† Calgon is the trade name for the chemical sodium hexametaphosphate which has the property of dispersing soil particles. Other water softeners—washing soda, which is sodium carbonate, and trisodium phosphate(TSP)—precipitate particles without first dispersing them and, therefore, cannot be used in this test.

Sedimentation Test

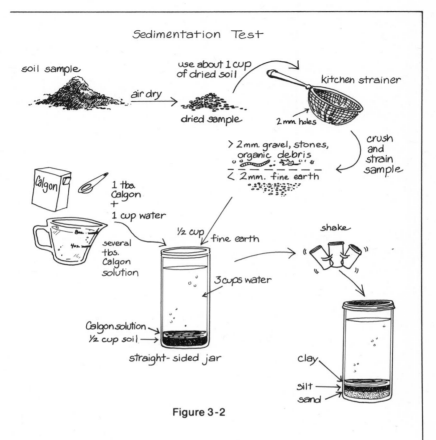

soil sample

air dry

use about 1 cup of dried soil

dried sample

kitchen strainer

2 mm. holes

crush and strain sample

> 2 mm. gravel, stones, organic debris

< 2 mm. fine earth

Calgon

1 tbs. Calgon + 1 cup water

several tbs. Calgon solution

½ cup fine earth

shake

3 cups water

Calgon solution ½ cup soil

straight-sided jar

clay

silt

sand

Figure 3-2

Sedimentation Test Record

time	millimeters

40 second measurement = mm. sand

30 minute measurement = mm. silt

12 hour measurement = total depth of mineral soil

sand layer _mm.
silt layer (30 minute measurement minus 40 second measurement)____mm.
clay layer (12 hour measurement minus 30 minute measurement)____mm.

$$\frac{sand\ depth}{total\ depth} \times 100 = \%\ sand \Big/ \frac{silt\ depth}{total\ depth} \times 100 = \%\ silt \Big/ \frac{clay\ depth}{total\ depth} \times 100 = \%\ clay$$

Figure 3-3

You will not get a correct reading if you wait 12 hours to take measurements of each of the layers because the textural classes grade into one another and your eye cannot precisely differentiate the sand from the silt or the silt from the clay.

In a soils laboratory the organic matter would be burned off in a muffle furnace. Since we cannot do that easily in our kitchen laboratories, the organic matter remains in the water suspension, some of it settling out after the mineral particles.

Box 3-4: Determining Soil Textures with the Feel Test

An experienced observer of soils can determine textural class by how the soil feels; try it yourself.

Sand grains can individually be seen or felt. When moist, sand forms a cast which crumbles on touch. If you squeeze dry sand in your hand, then open your hand and release pressure, the cast falls apart.

Sandy loam is held together by the small amounts of clay and silt present. Even the dry sandy loam soil forms a cast when squeezed, though it readily falls apart. A cast formed of moist soil, however, can be handled.

Loam feels somewhat gritty, but at the same time smooth and plastic. The cast formed by squeezing dry loam soil can bear careful handling while the cast of moist soil can be freely handled.

Silt has a floury, talcum powder feel when dry and is only moderately plastic and sticky when wet.

Silt loam may appear cloddy when dry, but the clods break easily. Wet soil runs together and puddles. Casts of wet or dry soil can be freely handled.

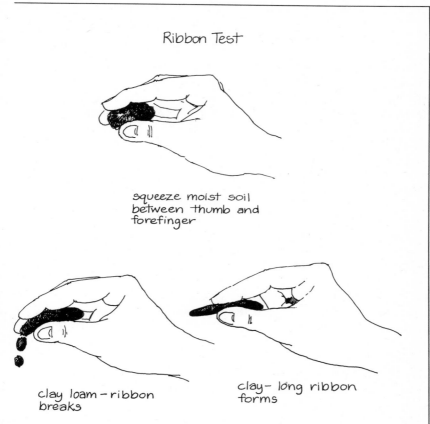

Ribbon Test

squeeze moist soil
between thumb and
forefinger

clay loam – ribbon
breaks

clay- long ribbon
forms

Figure 3-4

Clay loam breaks into clods which are hard when dry. When the soil is kneaded, it does not crumble, but works into a compact mass. If you do the "ribbon test"—moisten and squeeze a ball of soil between the thumb and forefinger—a short ribbon of soil is formed, but it breaks off easily under its own weight.

Clay is plastic and sticky when wet, forming hard lumps when dry. A long, flexible ribbon is formed by doing the "ribbon test" shown in Figure 3-4.

Sand particles are made of hard minerals and do not slough off much in the way of plant nutrients. The smaller silt particles are generally made of a more erodible material, so they contribute more mineral nutrients. The space between the silt particles is also smaller, and the water deposited there is able to resist the pull of gravity and remain available for plant use.

Clay particles are many times smaller than either sand or silt and are usually made of different material substances. The surface area of a small amount of clay is so great that this component of the soil is vitally important for the chemical retention of water and nutrient ions on its surfaces. Too much clay makes for a poor, wet soil, however. Organic matter in the soil plays a role similar to that of clay, but we are not able to measure how much of it there is in the soil with the sedimentation test. You can get a good idea of the amount of organic matter by feel—a crumbly, friable soil probably contains a high level of organic matter.

The USDA has created the Textural Triangle for easy determination of textural class once the percentage of each soil separate is known. "Loam," a term often misused to mean fertile soil, is actually the textural class representing a well-balanced mixture. The fact that the loamy soils are best for agriculture is no doubt how the misuse of the word came to be. As you can see from the Textural Triangle, this is not necessarily a mixture of even proportions, but a melding of the characteristics of the sand, silt, and clay into a soil that is not overwhelmed by any one of them.

Soil Moisture

"Field capacity" is the amount of water a soil can hold after it has been thoroughly wetted by rain or irrigation and the excess has drained off. It is the maximum amount of soil moisture available to plants, since water which drains off with the pull of gravity is in the root zone too briefly to be absorbed. Texture, structure, and amount of organic matter in a soil determine its field capacity.

As a soil dries out, it becomes more difficult for plant

(Continued on page 54)

Box 3-5: Textural Triangle

Once you know the proportion of sand, silt, and clay in your soil, you can use the Textural Triangle * to find out what to call the mixture. To use the Triangle (see Figure 3-5), draw a horizontal line across the Triangle from the percentage of clay which you found in your sample. Draw another line from the percentage of silt, this one parallel to the left side of the Triangle. These lines intercept in the box which gives the name of the correct textural class.

Textural Triangle

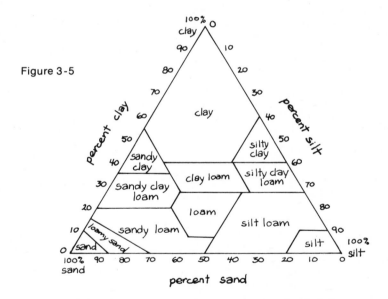

Figure 3-5

For example, if your soil is 35 percent clay and 30 percent silt, the two lines intercept in the box labeled "clay loam" (see Figure 3-6). Or if your soil is really quite sandy with only 10

(Continued)

* The Textural Triangle was prepared by the USDA Bureau of Plant Industry, Soils and Agricultural Engineering, May 1, 1950.

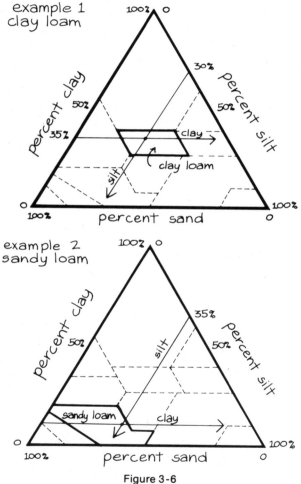

Examples of Soil Mixtures Identified
by Use of the Textural Triangle

example 1
clay loam

example 2
sandy loam

Figure 3-6

percent clay and 35 percent silt, the lines intercept in the box
labeled sandy loam (see Figure 3-6). You should add a lot of
organic matter to this soil to make up for its lack of clay.

Box 3-6: Measuring Soil Moisture

The size of the soil sample you should use depends in large part on the accuracy of your scales, since you will need to find the difference between the wet and dry weights. With a smaller sample, the test can be completed more rapidly as the smaller amount of soil dries out faster. If you have a fine balance, you can begin with perhaps four ounces of soil, but if you are relying on a bathroom or baby scale, you had better use a sample of about two pounds.

If you want to measure the maximum amount of water which your soil is capable of holding (this is called the field

(Continued)

Measuring Soil Moisture

time

(1) Preweigh container. _____ oz. _____

(2) Weigh soil sample in container. _____ oz. _____

(3) Subtract (1) from (2) for original weight. [_____ oz.] _____

(4) Dry soil in oven at 105°C. (221°F.) until you get
a constant weight. (When all the moisture has _____ oz. _____
evaporated and the soil is dry, the weight _____ oz. _____
no longer decreases. This may take 12 hours _____ oz. _____
or longer with a large sample.) Take it out _____ oz. _____
of the oven periodically for weighing and
record weights in the blanks on the right.

(5) Record final dry weight. _____ oz. _____

(6) Subtract (1) from (5) for dry weight of sample. [_____ oz.] _____

(7) Subtract dry weight (6) from wet weight (3)
to get the weight of water in the sample. [_____ oz.] _____

(8) Divide the weight of water (7) by the oven-
dry weight (6) and multiply by 100 to
get the percent soil moisture.

(Weight of water (7) ___ oz. ÷ oven-dry weight (6) ___ oz.) x 100 = ___ % soil moisture

Figure 3-7

capacity), slowly drip water over the surface of your sample. Periodically tilt the container holding the sample to see if the soil is saturated. Allow all the excess water to drain by holding the container at an angle. This process of bringing your soil to field capacity is not necessary if you just want to measure the percentage of moisture in your soil at a certain time.

To measure soil moisture percentage or field capacity, follow these steps and fill in the blanks as shown in Figure 3-7.

roots to collect the necessary moisture. The plant is under progressively greater stress until it reaches the point where it is losing more water to transpiration than it is able to get from the soil, and it wilts. You can measure the percentage of soil moisture at field capacity and then at progressively drier phases until the wilting point.

For more information about soils and soil testing, see Brady 1974, Foth 1978, Townsend 1973, Walsh and Beaton 1973, Yearbook of Agriculture 1938, and check the Soil Conservation Service publications about soils in your area.

Evaluating Natural Vegetation

Since, for the plant grower, the point of testing soil is to indicate how well a crop will do, another approach is to go directly to the plants to find out about the soil. The natural vegetation—both the species involved and the vitality of the growth—provides excellent indicators of soil fertility and suitability for garden or cropland. If there are inequalities in the land you plan to use for your experimental work, the vegetation already growing there can pinpoint the differences.

Cattails tell you it is too swampy; so do wet feet. Quack grass and chamomile indicate that drainage is poor due to a subsoil impenetrable layer. Lamb's-quarters and pigweed show up on a fertile soil. Where it is too acidic, you may find

(Continued on page 56)

Box 3-7: Measuring Plant and Leaf Surface Area

The basic idea is to count squares. You can do it using graph paper or using plastic or glass on which squares have been etched. Even a flexible sheet of plastic from a heavy-gauge plastic bag works fine. Using graph paper as a guide, rule in ½-cm. or 1-cm. squares. The scale depends on the size and complexity of the leaves or plant being measured (see Figure 3-8). Either etch in the squares with a carbide-tip scribe or draw them in with a ball-point pen.

You can take measurements in the field without destroying the plant by placing the plastic sheet (or glass or Plexiglas) over a plant and counting the number of squares which cover it. The size of individual leaves can be measured in the same way. An alternative is to draw an outline of the vegetation onto

(Continued)

Measuring Plant and Leaf Surface Area

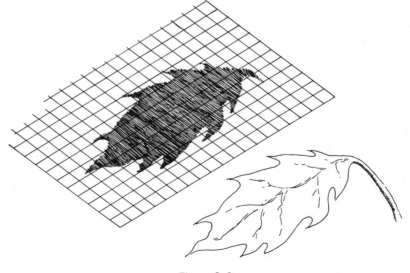

Figure 3-8

the plastic with a washable felt tip pen and count the number of squares within the outline at a later time.

Several other systems for estimating surface area have been developed by botanists and ecologists looking for a faster and less tedious method. Most of these call for either complex mathematics requiring a computer or expensive machines which electronically scan the surface area of the plant. This sample method seems the most appropriate, however, for those of us not planning on measuring surface area of vegetation too often.

cinquefoil and hawkweed, while on a limestone soil you might see cow cress.

Any of a number of plant and weed identification books can be used to identify these various plants. *A Field Guide to Wildflowers* (Peterson and McKenny 1968), part of the Peterson Field Guide Series, is quite complete and easy to use. Ehrenfried E. Pfeiffer's *Weeds and What They Tell* (1976) is particularly valuable for making connections between soil types and species which thrive on them.

Other helpful, nontechnical books which may be of help in identifying the natural vegetation in your area are Grimm 1968, Jaques 1958, and Meyer 1968. *Plant Ecology* (Weaver and Clements 1938) talks about vegetative indicators of different soil types and contains a wealth of other information on plant ecology.

Vegetational Quadrant Study

A systematic study of natural vegetation is more than you need to do as a preliminary for other gardening research, but it makes a fascinating ecological study in its own right.

Mark off an area and list or chart the species found in it (see Figure 3-9). Note how often each type of plant is seen. You can determine which of the plant species is dominant by picking and weighing sample plants. Another way to figure dominance is by measuring the surface area covered by each plant.

Constructing a Quadrant Plot for Systematic Study of Natural Vegetation

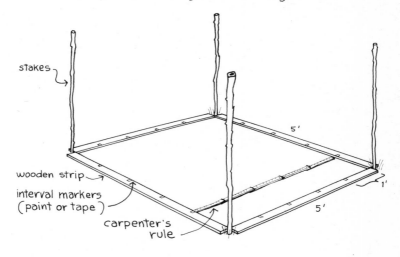

stakes

wooden strip
interval markers
(paint or tape)
carpenter's
rule

5'
1'
5'

Figure 3-9

To keep track of your study area so you can return throughout the growing season and watch the changes taking place, stake the four corners. So that you do not concentrate your efforts in some parts of the plot and leave out others, subdivide the area. Lay wooden strips marked at 6-inch or 1-foot intervals on the ground around the perimeter of the plot. Have another wooden strip, such as a folding carpenter's rule, long enough to stretch between the two sides of the plot. Place it at the first 6-inch or 1-foot marker and record or diagram all the plants found in that first strip. Then move the ruler down to the next marker, diagram those plants, and so on.

To diagram the plants growing in your study quadrant, use graph paper or paper onto which you have drawn perpendicular, intersecting lines to scale. A scale of 10:1 is useful for most types of vegetation, but if there is very dense growth a scale of 5:1 may be preferable. That means for a

5-foot x 5-foot plot your chart should be 6 inches x 6 inches on a 10:1 scale or 12 inches x 12 inches with a 5:1 ratio.

You will need a system for diagraming the location and size of each type of plant. Make up one of your own or follow my suggestions (see Figure 3-10). Where there is a stem, draw a small circle and then use a dotted line to indicate the span of the plant. The size of the circles should be proportional to the size of the stems. If several stems come from the same root base, you can either draw in that many circles or write in the number of stems. Measure and write in the height of the plant. Where vegetation is very thick, instead of drawing in each plant separately, indicate the various plant types with hatch marks oriented in different directions.

If you do not know the identification of the plant at this point, make a key. Take a sample, label it with the same letter you use on the chart, and write a description while the plant is still fresh. If you intend to study this same area later in the season, try to get your live plant sample from an adjacent piece of land, leaving your plot intact.

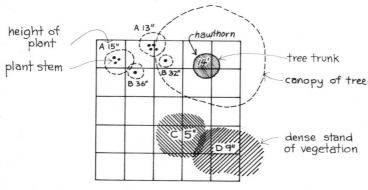

Sample Diagram Showing the Location and Size of Plants Growing in a Quadrant Plot

Figure 3-10

Experimental Field Showing
Transect Line across Diagonal

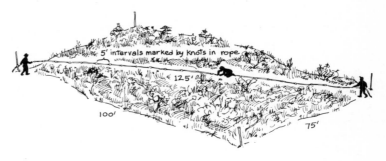

Figure 3-11

Transect Line

When you want to get a sense of soil differences over a large expanse of land, sampling with a transect line may be preferable to the intensive study of a small plot as just described. Use a tape or rope with markings at intervals and stretch it out over a predetermined patch on your land (see Figure 3-11). At the intervals marked, sample plants on one or both sides of the tape, depending on the detail desired. The spacing between markings is also very much a matter of choice as to how much detail you want.

Identifying the sampled plants is an exciting project in its own right. It is easier to identify the plants when they are fresh, but if you cannot do that for some reason or if you want to preserve the plants for future reference, you can make a simple plant press to dry your samples and keep them in good condition. Write some notes as to the appearance of the living plant and when and where it was found, because the dried plant will not look quite like it did when it was fresh. Use plant identification books to make your determinations, or ask your county agent or a botanist at a local college for suggestions for finding a plant taxonomist to help you.

(Continued on page 65)

59

Box 3-8: Drying and Pressing Plants

Plants can be picked and preserved for identification and then kept for a reference collection. Pick small plants whole. For larger plants, just take a selection of leaves from the top, middle, and basal portions along with a sample of the flower or fruit.

You can buy a plant press from a biological supply house or you can make one yourself. The wooden portions of the press are made by nailing wooden battens 1 inch x ¼ inch to cross-strips with ⅜-inch tacks, as pictured in Figure 3-12. The frame can be of any size. You will need two of these sections, one for the top and one for the bottom of the press.

Dr. Mildred Faust, a very knowledgeable plant taxonomist who is the source of many of these hints for pressing plants, says that while this cross-wood construction is recommended for good air circulation, you can use plywood or a large, heavy book, such as a dictionary, "even though it doesn't do the dictionary any good after a while."

Above the wooden base put a sheet of corrugated cardboard cut and placed so that the corrugations run the short

Wooden Frame for Plant Press

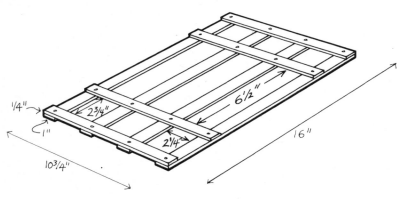

Figure 3-12

way. Cut these from a cardboard box or get them from a supply house. Next, lay in a sheet of blotting paper or several sheets of newspaper. The plant specimen follows, placed inside a folded sheet of newspaper. With it, put a label with collection information: date, place, and description of the habitat. Now reverse the order and put the blotting paper or newspaper above the specimen, then the corrugated cardboard, and finally the other half of the wooden frame.

You can press a number of plants simultaneously, by separating them with blotting paper or newspaper sheets (see Figure 3-13).

The whole arrangement is then weighted down with rocks or books, or is strapped together with adjustable straps which should be tightened periodically during the drying process. Webbed camping straps—the kind used to attach tents and sleeping bags to backpacks—are perfect for the job.

The press can simply be left in a relatively dry room or it can be placed over a radiator or near low-wattage bulbs (10 to 15 watts). Color is supposedly better retained if the plants are dried with a heat source. An oven is too difficult to regulate at low temperatures, however, and should *not* be used.

(Continued)

Using the Plant Press

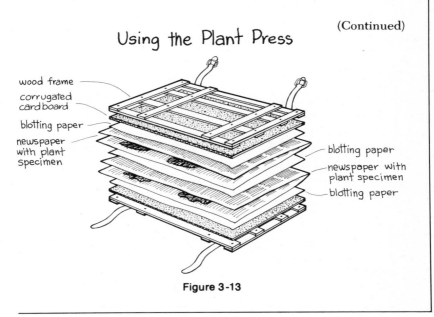

wood frame
corrugated cardboard
blotting paper
newspaper with plant specimen

blotting paper
newspaper with plant specimen
blotting paper

Figure 3-13

Padding Bulky Plant Parts with Folded Paper before Pressing

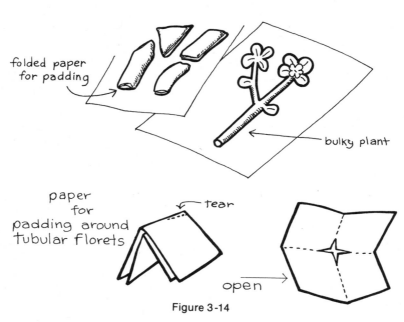

folded paper for padding

bulky plant

paper for padding around tubular florets

tear

open →

Figure 3-14

After the first 24 hours of pressing, your plants will still be soft enough to manipulate. Open the press and arrange the specimens in the way you would like them to look permanently. For example, at least one leaf should be top side up and another bottom side up. The blotting paper or newspaper above, below, and between specimens should be changed at this time. How long the plants take to dry varies with the weather, the plants involved, and the source of drying heat.

Some plants need special attention: to stop succulents from continuing to grow while they are being pressed, they should first be dipped in boiling water. Their stems can be cut in half lengthwise to reduce bulkiness. Put padding around bulky plant parts to equalize the pressure (see Figure 3-14). Otherwise, thicker areas will become squashed. The padding should go between two sheets of drying paper rather than flush against the plant.

Flowers with central tubular florets, such as daisies, can be protected in a different way. Fold a piece of paper the size of the flower into quarters, then make a small tear in both directions at the junction of the folds. Open the paper and place it over the flower so that the tube petals project through the hole as shown in Figure 3-14.

When the plant is completely dry, transfer it to "herbarium paper," which is quality paper with a high rag content chosen for its longevity. Hold the plant down to the paper at a few strategic locations with a cloth tape such as adhesive tape. The tape can either be attached flush with the plant and paper or it can be made to bridge the plant so that it does not actually touch but merely confines it (see Figure 3-15). This avoids damage in case you want to remove the plant from the herbarium sheet, but leaves open the possibility that, if the bridge is too loose, the dried plant can rattle about and, perhaps, break.

A full label belongs in the lower left corner of the herbarium sheet with the family, generic, and specific names of the plant, its common names, the locality and habitat where found, date when found, name of collector, and collection number.

Tape Bridge

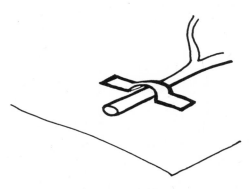

Figure 3-15

Box 3-9: Preserving Plants in Liquid

Plants can also be immersed in preservation fluid and stored in jars. Nonsucculent herbaceous plants need a solution of 70 to 95 percent ethyl or isopropyl alcohol, both known as rubbing alcohol and available in drugstores. Succulent plants which contain much water in their cells require a 2 to 5 percent formalin preservation fluid. The following standard formula (Purvis et al. 1964) combining these two preservative bases works best for many plants: 15 parts alcohol; 10 parts distilled water; 1 part commercial formalin; and 1 part glacial acetic acid.

Wash all grit and gummy residues off the specimens and then mount them on glass slabs using thread or nonsoluble glue. Put the slabs into jars filled with the preservative as shown in Figure 3-16; then seal them to prevent evaporation.

A freezer can be used for short-term storage of flowers. Just pack the loose, fresh flowers in plastic bags and freeze them.

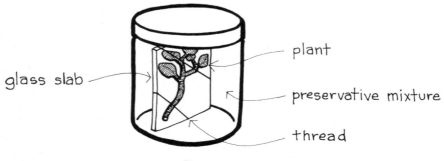

Liquid Preservation of Plant Specimen

glass slab

plant

preservative mixture

thread

Figure 3-16

Uniformity Trials and Soil Fertility Maps

If you are planning to conduct an extensive experiment, you may be interested in carrying out a uniformity trial and then mapping the results in a soil fertility map. A uniformity trial is a direct way to find out if the conditions over your entire experimental site are equal or, if not equal, how they vary. To conduct a uniformity trial, plant the same crop in the same density over the entire area and proceed to treat it equally for the duration of the growing season. In other words, do not water or fertilize one part of the trial area and not another.

<u>Diagram of a Uniformity Trial Plot</u> showing a 1 acre field planted in barley and divided into 100 subplots

yields row totals (lbs.)

	1	2	3	4	5	6	7	8	9	10	
52.1	5.5	5.4	5.9	5.9	5.6	5.2	5.0	4.6	4.6	4.4	— subplot yield (lbs.)
	11	12	13	14	15	16	17	18	19	20	
51.0	5.6	5.3	5.7	5.6	5.4	5.1	5.0	4.6	4.4	4.3	— subplot number
	21	22	23	24	25	26	27	28	29	30	
49.7	4.4	4.9	4.8	4.7	5.3	5.0	5.3	5.2	5.0	5.1	
	31	32	33	34	35	36	37	38	39	40	
48.1	4.4	4.5	4.5	4.4	4.7	4.8	5.2	5.4	5.1	5.1	
	41	42	43	44	45	46	47	48	49	50	
46.9	4.0	3.3	4.1	4.2	4.4	4.9	5.1	5.3	5.7	5.9	
	51	52	53	54	55	56	57	58	59	60	
46.6	3.8	3.4	3.7	4.1	4.5	5.1	5.2	5.1	5.8	5.9	
	61	62	63	64	65	66	67	68	69	70	
49.0	4.3	3.8	4.1	4.4	4.6	5.2	5.6	5.5	5.7	5.8	
	71	72	73	74	75	76	77	78	79	80	
52.9	4.9	4.8	4.9	4.8	5.1	5.5	5.7	6.1	5.5	5.6	
	81	82	83	84	85	86	87	88	89	90	
53.6	4.8	4.9	4.8	4.7	5.2	5.4	5.8	6.1	6.0	5.9	
	91	92	93	94	95	96	97	98	99	100	
50.1	4.8	4.8	4.9	4.2	4.5	5.0	5.1	5.8	5.5	5.5	

yield column totals (lbs.)

	46.5	45.1	47.4	47.0	49.3	51.2	53.0	53.7	53.3	53.5

total yield = 500 lbs.
mean yield = 5.0 lbs.

Figure 3-17

65

Partition the trial area into small subplots which are numbered and staked for identification. Prepare a diagram of the partitioned area. When it comes time to harvest, record the yield from each of the subplots separately. Differences in yield indicate unequal growing conditions, primarily inequalities in soil fertility but perhaps also in site orientation or altitude.

It is especially valuable to conduct a uniformity trial before embarking on a long-term project where the same plots would be in use for a number of years. It is also important if you are planning to carry out part of the experiment in your backyard (or field) and part in someone else's. The data from the two sites should not be pooled unless the growing conditions are similar.

The diagram of a one-acre barley field partitioned into 100 subplots, shown in Figure 3-17, illustrates a uniformity trial. The total yield for the acre is a hypothetical 500 pounds, so the average yield per subplot is 5 pounds. You could try to picture the soil gradients from the information shown in the diagram or you could make a soil fertility map to illustrate it graphically.

To make a soil fertility map begin by diagraming the area tested as shown in Figure 3-17. Figure the average yield of the subplots and then establish "yield classes." For the example shown in the illustration, the yield classes are:

greater than 15% of the mean yield . . . . . . >5.75 lbs.
5 to 15% more than the mean yield . . 5.25–5.75 lbs.
±5% of the mean yield. . . . . 4.75–5.25 lbs.
5 to 15% less than the mean yield . . . 4.25–4.75 lbs.
more than 15% less than the mean yield . . 4.25 lbs.

(The amounts in pounds are arrived at by multiplying the percentage, say 15%, by the mean yield, which in this case is 5 pounds [0.15 × 5 = 0.75], and adding the result to the mean yield [5 pounds + 0.75 pounds = 5.75 pounds].)

Your map is made by drawing in contour lines—as in a topographic map. Whereas on a topographic map the contour lines mark off ranges in elevation, here they mark off ranges in yield. Look at the yields given for two adjacent subplots (see Figure 3-18). If one is greater than the amount demarcating a yield class and the other is less, then you know that a contour line must be drawn somewhere between the two. Assume that the yield for a subplot occurs at the center of the subplot and then grades into the yields found for adjacent plots. Thus the yield at the boundary between subplots is always the average between the two.

Let us begin to draw the map by finding the first point on a contour line indicating 5.75 pounds. Look at plots 90 and 100: the yield at the border between them is 5.7 pounds, so the point through which the contour line passes is above the border in plot 90. Moving on to the next two plots, numbers 89 and 99, with yields of 6.0 and 5.5 pounds respectively, place the point right on the subplot boundary line. The contour line does not continue between plots 88 and 98 since both of these had yields greater than 5.75 pounds. Rather it is drawn down between plots 98 and 99, close to the center of plot 98. To figure how to "turn the corner," average the yields between two diagonal plots and draw in the point accordingly.

Continue this process, working on one contour line at a

Drawing in the Points to Make Contour Lines on the Soil Fertility Map

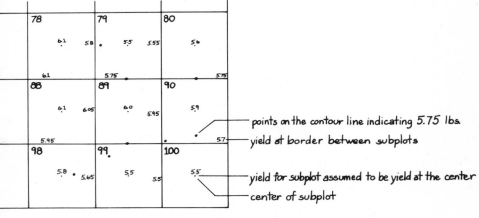

Figure 3-18

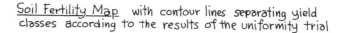

Soil Fertility Map with contour lines separating yield classes according to the results of the uniformity trial

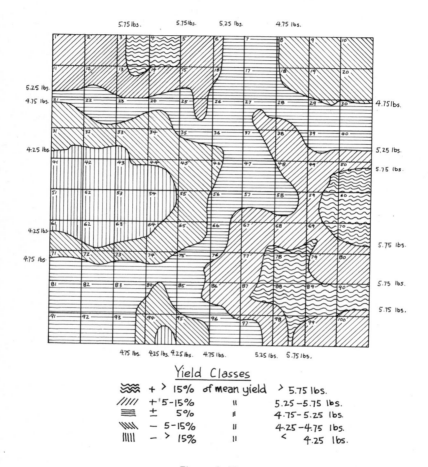

Figure 3-19

time, until all the points for one line have been marked. Then draw in a smooth contour line by connecting the points. When the process has been completed for all the lines, you will have an attractive, but abstract, illustration (see Figure 3-19). The final step is to make sense of your work of art and to put it to use in deciding how to place your experimental plots to best compensate for soil irregularities.

Compensating for Soil Irregularities

Soil irregularities can be dealt with either by decreasing the differences or by manipulating the experimental design to make the inequalities less significant. Compost is said to be the great equalizer in a garden since it uniformly increases the amount of organic matter. A cover crop or green manure plowed back into the land has the same leveling effect on a larger field.

When plants are under stress, differences in soil quality become more apparent. Thus, you should use disease-resistant plants and give them sufficient moisture and fertilization unless one of these is the factor which you are testing.

EXPERIMENTAL PLOTS

The size, shape, number, and placement of plots also compensate for soil irregularities. Usually soil quality changes in a gradual but unpredictable pattern so that the researcher must assign plots randomly to avoid biasing the experiment. But sometimes a gardener or farmer can be quite certain that he or she has a field with a soil-quality gradient running in just one direction. A hillside garden is a good example because, unless great care has been taken, it is likely that over the years erosion has carried the best soil from the top of the field to the flatland at the bottom. These situations can be compensated for with long, narrow plots running in the direction of the greatest variation (see Figure 3-20). In this way no one treatment has the advantage of the best soil or the disadvantage of the worst. This same arrangement would be used if one experiment were to follow another where, for example, different amounts of fertilizer were added. The plots for the second experiment should be laid at right angles to those of the first (see Figure 3-21).

Long plots are also well suited to the needs of farm

Plot Layout on a Hillside

Place the plots so that no one of them has the advantage of being on the best soil or the disadvantage of being on the poorest soil.

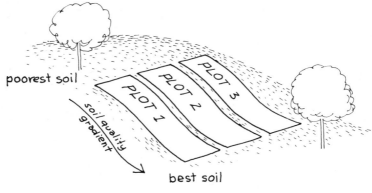

poorest soil

soil quality gradient

best soil

Figure 3-20

Plot Layout When the Same Soil Is Used for an Experiment More Than Once

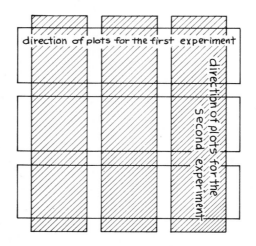

direction of plots for the first experiment

direction of plots for the second experiment

Figure 3-21

machinery, but these advantages must be weighed against the disadvantages of having an extended border (see Figure 3-22). Plants along the edge of a plot have a different "lifestyle" than those in the center.

Border Effect

Along an alleyway or edge of a field, plants have the advantage of greater access to the sun's rays and no neighbors on one side to compete with for food and water. Those plants bordering on another plot, however, have to contend with the needs and habits of the adjoining plants which may compete with their own. Also, if the neighboring plots are being watered or fertilized in different amounts, it is difficult to contain the effects of these treatments within their designated plot boundaries.

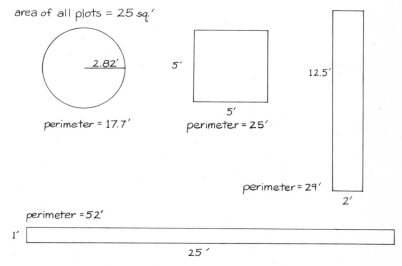

Plot Area Vs. Perimeter

The more linear the plot, the longer the border will be. With a longer border a greater percentage of the crop must be disregarded due to the border effect.

area of all plots = 25 sq.'

2.82'

perimeter = 17.7'

5'

5'

perimeter = 25'

12.5'

perimeter = 29'

2'

perimeter = 52'

1'

25'

Figure 3-22

The Border Effect

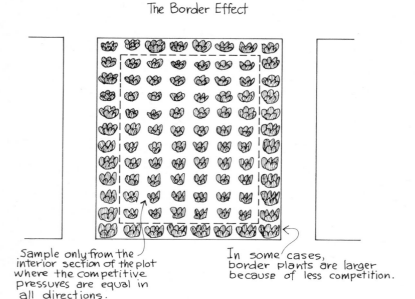

Sample only from the
interior section of the plot
where the competitive
pressures are equal in
all directions.

In some cases,
border plants are larger
because of less competition.

Figure 3-23

Thus it is common practice, when collecting data from an experimental plot, to disregard plants along the borders and on the ends of rows (see Figure 3-23). This is done even though during the course of the experiment you have treated these plants the same as all the others in the plot. Plots must, therefore, be wide enough to allow for border plants while still leaving at least one row in the middle from which to draw your sample.

The other alternative, which only works for very large field plots, is to disregard the border effect on the assumption that when all the plants are averaged together, the border effect will be negligible.

Competition among plants is greatest when moisture is a limiting factor. Plants with the same needs, such as those of the same species, are the most voracious competitors. So to best regulate competition and make the conditions most similar to what the plants are already facing within their own plots, it is best to group plots of plants with similar moisture needs and maturation dates. For experimental purposes do not have a plot of pumpkins, for example, next to one of beets because the pumpkins will behave differently next to the beets than next to the other pumpkins with which they are being compared. Another way to reduce inequalities, both within and between plots, is to conduct your experiment away from trees, hedgerows, and buildings.

Intraplot Competition

The results of an experiment will also differ depending on the competition a plant faces within its own plot due to spacing between plants and overall density. To best regulate both of these factors, the plot should be overplanted and then thinned as desired.

Strong or fast-growing plants have a competitive advantage over smaller plants as shown dramatically in a 1923 experiment with corn. When large and small varieties were planted in the same hill, the yield of the small variety was 47 percent of the larger; when they were planted in alternate rows, the yield was 66 percent; but when planted in separate plots, the yield was 85 percent of the larger (Kiesselbach 1923).

Plot Size and Plot Replications

There are two categories of experimental plots: "nursery plots" which are small and cared for by hand, and "field plots" which are large enough to be cared for by standard farm machinery.

Just how large an experimental plot should be depends on the type of crop as well as on the degree of accuracy required. Plants with the greatest individual variability need larger plots so the full range of genetic possibilities is more likely to be represented.

Trees have the greatest individual variability and a recommended size for plots of an established tree crop is about 1/10 acre (Jeffers 1960). For most vegetable crops, 1/1,000 acre, which is about 44 square feet, is a good size. (Open-pollinated crops, however, need a bigger plot due to greater variability.) Nursery seedlings require less space—perhaps a square yard.

These sizes are mentioned merely to put you into the right ball park, because there is no one correct size for an experimental plot. Many studies have been done to arrive at an ideal plot size for specific crops, though no two studies seem to come up with the same results. An "ideal-size plot" is one which has the most consistent results when the experiment is repeated: large enough to grow the number of plants needed to represent the diversity of the stock, while small enough to avoid the problems created by soil heterogeneity. The data collected from a plot that is too large are too variable; therefore, the results may not be sufficiently precise to compare with those from another treatment plot.

Studies have shown that plots larger than 1/40 acre, which is about 1,100 square feet, are already too big for agricultural experiments (Mercer and Hall 1911). The same amount of land is better utilized when divided into smaller plots which repeat or "replicate" the experiment.

Replications are duplications over time and/or space. Experiments are replicated because measurements of samples drawn from the trial material differ in unpredictable and often uncontrollable ways. Sometimes samples show better results than can realistically be expected from the treatment as a whole, and sometimes the results are worse. When data collected from all the replications of one treatment are considered together, the chance variations incurred by any one of the treatments are balanced out.

If you were to conduct an experiment in which you irrigate one plot of carrots but not another, you would expect that the results (measured in terms of the size of the carrots) would reflect the effects of watering on carrots in general. The experiment would not be worth much if you could only count on it to show the effects of watering on the particular carrots which you measured for your sample. You expect, in other words, to be able to generalize from your sample, to be able to make some predictions as to whether irrigation does or does not affect the size of carrots.

This would be easy if all carrots responded to irrigation with a consistent increase in size. Then you could definitely say whether watering carrots does in fact increase their yield significantly. But due to the types of variation we have been discussing (in the weather, in plant genes, and in soil), this is not the case. Even if the carrots do increase in size with watering, the size of each carrot and the amount of the increase vary.

If you have just one plot for each treatment, with no replications, you will just have one set of results. You will have no way of knowing how close your sample is to being representative of the average carrot because you have no basis for computing what the average is. By replicating the experiment, you can collect several sets of data and use them to compute both the average size and the deviation from that size which would still be considered within the normal range for a particular treatment. With this information you can compare the effects of different treatments, as we show in Chapter 9.

The American Society of Agronomy recommends three to six replicates for each treatment, with a few more if the plots are small or if they are spread out over a number of different locations. When the replications are all in the same field, the variability among them is not likely to be as great as it would be if they were scattered over several backyards or fields. This is because the soil and weather conditions tend to be similar on adjacent lands.

The effects of the experimental treatments can be more precisely defined and differentiated when the variability among replicates is small. In other words, if the sizes of all your samples of irrigated carrots were very similar and the sizes of all the nonirrigated carrots were also similar, then you would be able to say with confidence whether or not irrigating makes a difference in the size of carrots.

Sometimes, however, due to lack of space in a single backyard or because the researcher wants to see the more general effect of a treatment under somewhat different conditions, the replications are spread out and placed in different backyards and fields. When this happens, there is likely to be a greater variation among replications. This causes the data to be more variable and, thus, causes the conclusions to be less precise. There would have to be larger differences between the effects of the treatments (e.g., the size of the carrots) in order for the researcher to draw the conclusion that the treatment (e.g., irrigating) did indeed make a difference.

Data from scattered replications can be pooled as long as the differences in the growing conditions are not too great, the plots are of the same size, the same number of sampling units is chosen randomly from each plot and, most importantly, the experiment is carried out in exactly the same way in each location. When data from different locations are pooled in this way, it is best to have from 15 to 30 replicates of the experiment (Hopp 1954).

Plots can be arranged relative to one another in several different "experimental designs." These designs and their relative advantages are what we shall be talking about next.

EXPERIMENTAL DESIGNS

Good experimental designs carefully place plots of appropriate size and shape relative to one another. In situations where soil conditions are known to vary in just one direction, as in the example given previously of the hillside garden, it is possible to use certain systematic (nonrandom) designs, such as the half-drill method of replication or the balanced method of plot layout and replication. In most cases, however, it is preferable to use one of the "randomized designs," such as the completely random, the randomized block, the Latin square, or the split plot. Examples of each of these will be shown.

The **half-drill method of replication** is especially suited for field plot experiments comparing two varieties of a crop like corn when the planting is done with standard farm machinery. Seed of one variety is put in half the drill box and seed of another is put in the other half (see Figure 3-24). The resultant narrow plots present some harvesting difficulties and complications vis-à-vis border effects. There are, however, the compensations of easy planting and of being able to compare yields of the two varieties as they are grown side by side.

The **balanced method of plot layout and replication** is

Half-Drill Method of Replication: comparing 2 varieties of corn in 4 replications on an experimental field with a soil gradient in 1 direction only

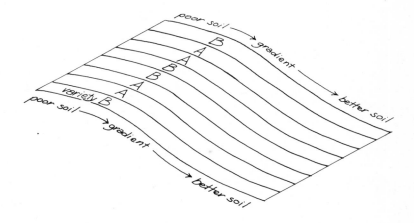

Figure 3-24

intended to be laid out as shown in Figure 3-25, with the distance from the center of the field to one of the three replicated plots equal to the sum of the distances of the other two replicates in the opposite direction. It is suited for a soil with a uniform gradation.

Randomization

Other than the preceding two designs, most experimental designs randomly place the plots in one of the various patterns to be described shortly. Conditions of random choice are met if all the alternatives have an equal chance of being used. Thus you can do your random choosing by throwing dice, shuffling cards, or picking numbers out of a hat. If you keep doing this and write down the numbers picked, you are in effect compiling a "random number table." Fortunately for those of us with other ways to spend our time, quite a few random number tables of various types

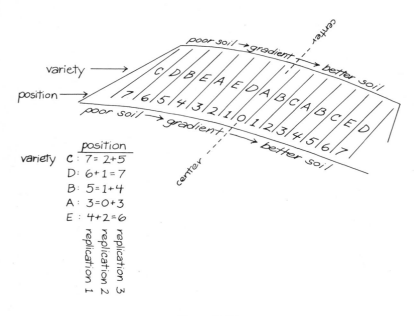

Figure 3-25

have been generated by a computer and are reprinted in statistics books.

An example of a computer-generated random number table, called a Table of Random Permutations, and good for up to 16 variables, is illustrated in Box 3-10. In this type of table each number is used just once in each column, so the table must be read vertically. Another type of table, the Table of Random Digits, is illustrated in Box 3-11. It is used for randomizing any number of variables and is especially valuable for "sampling with replacement," when the same item can be chosen more than once.

To see how the Table of Random Permutations is used in laying out plots, assume that you are doing an experiment comparing yields of four varieties of cabbage with three replications, for a total of 12 plots. For the experimental site let us use the top strip of the acre of land on which the

(Continued on page 80)

Box 3-10: Table of Random Permutations

Permutations of 16

7	12	15	15	1	2	7	16	10	2	14	15	7	13	13	10	6	1	8	10
13	3	8	16	7	10	11	10	13	5	11	7	13	16	7	7	5	13	2	14
3	1	4	5	14	13	3	14	9	13	13	2	9	15	6	2	8	4	5	8
11	8	16	14	15	6	2	6	2	16	8	5	12	3	9	13	4	3	10	4
14	9	1	6	3	9	14	13	8	6	5	8	14	7	3	15	13	11	4	7
2	16	10	13	5	5	13	2	11	7	3	12	5	14	12	16	2	2	9	15
4	6	13	7	2	15	1	9	1	4	7	10	6	9	11	9	7	6	16	11
6	14	6	10	4	14	4	15	3	3	4	16	2	6	5	1	12	10	6	9
10	15	2	1	13	12	16	3	4	8	10	1	15	5	14	12	14	12	3	2
12	10	7	12	9	11	9	8	12	14	15	4	11	8	16	8	9	14	14	1
15	7	5	2	10	7	8	12	6	15	6	13	16	12	15	4	11	8	12	6
16	2	11	8	8	8	15	5	16	1	1	9	8	1	8	14	16	5	13	5
9	13	14	3	6	4	10	11	5	12	9	3	10	4	4	3	10	9	1	3
8	11	9	4	11	3	12	7	7	10	12	14	3	10	1	6	15	16	15	12
1	5	12	11	16	16	5	4	14	9	16	11	1	2	10	5	1	15	7	13
5	4	3	9	12	1	6	1	15	11	2	6	4	11	2	11	3	7	11	16

11	8	16	5	5	13	1	13	2	16	14	12	9	8	7	5	13	3	13	3
2	2	8	8	14	16	4	3	8	11	10	14	15	1	2	11	4	5	15	9
6	13	2	13	6	5	9	15	11	10	12	6	16	15	16	9	10	12	16	15
14	12	4	16	16	11	14	10	5	12	3	3	12	14	15	13	6	4	1	16
8	6	3	9	4	10	6	4	16	2	2	9	8	16	4	6	5	15	7	8
9	15	12	10	3	2	12	6	1	15	4	13	7	7	9	12	14	8	8	11
3	10	11	12	13	12	5	11	7	8	9	5	14	11	10	1	3	13	3	5
16	1	13	14	8	14	15	5	3	7	11	15	6	12	5	7	11	1	14	4
1	14	14	2	9	15	16	14	6	14	7	8	3	13	11	8	7	7	12	7
4	4	6	4	12	3	11	8	15	9	8	1	13	6	3	3	15	9	9	12
15	5	1	11	10	6	3	7	10	5	5	11	10	10	12	15	16	14	5	2
5	3	5	6	7	7	13	2	14	3	16	4	5	5	13	4	9	16	2	6
12	7	15	15	15	9	8	12	12	13	15	10	1	4	6	16	2	6	11	1
10	11	10	3	2	4	2	1	4	6	6	7	11	9	14	10	8	11	4	13
7	9	7	7	11	1	7	16	13	1	13	2	4	2	1	2	12	2	10	14
13	16	9	1	1	8	10	9	9	4	1	16	2	3	8	14	1	10	6	10

1	6	7	4	8	6	5	2	8	15	4	6	6	1	4	5	7	13	2	10
9	15	11	3	11	15	9	10	1	3	8	2	15	7	9	8	16	1	14	3
10	16	4	5	12	9	16	11	7	1	7	16	11	8	3	3	12	2	3	4
4	14	1	9	5	5	4	13	6	8	15	5	12	5	7	16	5	11	8	1
7	3	13	14	15	2	1	14	16	5	14	9	2	16	1	12	6	14	4	13
16	11	2	1	14	16	6	9	3	4	16	14	3	15	11	11	3	9	12	5
3	10	16	16	13	7	13	1	11	14	9	10	16	2	10	2	10	7	10	16
11	13	9	13	4	13	8	3	5	13	10	12	5	12	5	14	13	16	5	6
15	2	3	12	9	12	2	4	13	10	3	13	14	4	2	1	14	8	6	12
14	1	14	6	10	1	3	12	4	2	2	4	13	3	16	9	9	3	7	14
13	12	5	11	3	11	15	8	2	7	11	7	8	14	12	4	4	4	15	11
12	5	10	7	2	14	7	15	14	16	13	1	9	10	12	10	11	10	9	8
8	9	8	10	6	4	11	7	10	11	6	8	4	9	14	15	8	6	11	9
2	7	6	2	1	8	10	6	15	12	1	11	7	11	13	6	1	15	13	15
6	4	15	8	16	10	14	16	9	6	12	3	10	6	14	7	2	12	16	7
5	8	12	15	7	3	12	5	12	9	5	15	1	13	15	13	15	5	1	2

13	4	10	4	16	13	16	13	5	3	6	14	1	16	8	7	2	3	3	12
5	14	4	6	8	2	15	1	13	14	16	4	15	4	3	12	12	1	4	7
2	2	2	15	14	16	9	12	16	6	10	15	14	9	10	1	14	8	8	16
7	12	15	8	12	3	5	14	7	12	5	13	16	1	7	5	11	2	9	3
6	9	7	14	9	14	10	11	15	11	12	1	12	12	14	16	3	11	11	8
14	5	16	7	10	8	11	8	14	13	7	11	6	3	11	4	4	6	6	9
15	11	8	9	7	12	8	7	1	15	9	3	3	7	13	11	10	4	5	1
11	6	6	1	4	1	3	16	12	5	4	9	13	13	6	8	15	9	1	14
4	10	3	16	2	11	7	9	6	9	1	8	4	11	5	2	16	10	12	4
1	8	1	13	1	15	4	4	11	4	2	16	5	8	1	9	5	12	16	6
9	7	14	2	6	4	14	10	9	8	15	10	7	10	9	10	6	14	10	11
12	1	9	10	15	5	2	15	10	2	14	2	8	2	4	13	8	5	15	5
3	3	12	11	5	9	6	6	3	10	13	12	9	6	2	15	7	15	7	13
10	15	11	5	13	7	12	5	2	7	11	5	10	15	3	3	1	13	13	10
8	13	13	3	3	10	13	2	4	1	8	6	11	14	15	6	9	16	2	2
16	16	5	12	11	6	1	3	8	16	3	7	2	5	16	14	13	7	14	15

Source: Cochran and Cox 1957.

uniformity trial was run since we already have a soil fertility map of the area.

Give each treatment an identifying symbol: C_1 equals variety 1; C_2 equals variety 2; C_3 equals variety 3; C_4 equals variety 4. The first step in using the Table of Random Permutations is to decide which block of numbers to use. We can either start with the first block and methodically work our way across the table, using a different set of numbers for each randomization, or we can pick two numbers between 1 and 4 as coordinates to pinpoint one of the blocks on the table. If we choose the numbers 4 and 4, we count four blocks over from the left and four blocks down from the top and find ourselves looking at the block in the lower right-hand corner of the page. The first column of numbers reads: 7, 12, 1, 5, 16, 4, 11, 8, 2, 9, 10, 13, 15, 3, 6, 14. By going through the four treatments in rotation three times and discarding the numbers between 13 and 16 (since we are randomizing a total of 12 plots), the treatments are assigned to plots in the order shown below:

$$7—C_1$$
$$12—C_2$$
$$1—C_3$$
$$5—C_4$$
$$16—\text{discard}$$
$$4—C_1$$
$$11—C_2$$
$$8—C_3$$
$$2—C_4$$
$$9—C_1$$
$$10—C_2$$
$$13—\text{discard}$$
$$15—\text{discard}$$
$$3—C_3$$
$$6—C_4$$
$$14—\text{discard}$$

Variety C_1 is planted in the first plot chosen, variety C_2 in the next, and so on as illustrated.

(Continued on page 82)

Box 3-11: Table of Random Digits

The following instructions and table are from Little and Hills 1975.

To randomize any set of ten items or less, begin at a random point on the table and follow either rows, columns, or diagonals in either direction. Write down the numbers in the order they appear, disregarding those which are higher than the number being randomized and those which have appeared before in the series. If you wish to randomize more than ten numbers, pairs of columns or rows can be combined to form two-digit numbers and the same process followed as that described above.

```
8 2 0 3 1 4 5 8 2 1 7 2 7 3 8 5 5 2 9 0 6 3 1 6 4
0 8 7 3 3 1 9 7 5 2 5 7 6 9 8 0 3 6 2 5 1 2 7 5 2
2 3 3 8 6 1 4 2 4 0 2 6 1 8 9 5 2 6 9 8 3 4 0 1 0
4 7 5 5 6 3 0 7 7 1 9 1 6 1 7 4 1 7 1 3 7 9 3 3 7
1 9 3 9 5 3 4 9 5 5 2 7 5 8 0 3 4 8 8 1 2 7 5 3 4
2 8 7 8 1 4 1 4 9 4 2 4 1 5 2 9 4 6 2 1 5 2 8 1 9
8 4 8 5 1 3 9 6 6 0 7 2 1 9 0 2 0 6 7 0 6 0 1 3 0
0 3 8 8 4 7 5 1 5 1 7 3 4 5 2 0 7 4 7 9 6 6 7 7 4
3 5 3 1 9 3 7 4 9 5 0 2 0 1 4 6 2 5 4 5 8 5 0 9 2
3 4 5 9 5 2 7 9 8 9 0 5 5 8 5 1 7 7 3 5 5 4 7 7 2
4 1 5 3 0 9 1 3 7 2 5 8 7 7 1 3 6 3 9 7 8 7 9 1 7
7 2 9 5 6 7 8 5 4 5 3 4 5 4 1 9 8 6 7 5 7 9 3 1 8
5 9 2 8 9 8 6 4 4 1 5 3 7 7 0 8 0 2 5 6 0 6 1 2 0
1 3 3 3 9 0 5 2 8 7 4 0 9 0 3 7 3 1 7 9 4 5 5 2 8
4 6 0 1 0 8 6 2 1 0 0 5 0 3 1 5 4 9 0 3 7 4 7 0 1
7 7 0 6 6 3 2 8 8 5 8 9 5 6 4 0 5 9 1 8 0 5 4 9 4
3 3 8 5 7 5 7 4 3 4 5 7 9 6 9 5 0 7 7 6 6 8 8 5 9
9 1 7 1 3 6 9 2 9 1 9 4 2 3 3 0 8 1 8 7 7 6 4 7 2
6 2 2 8 0 9 4 5 3 7 2 5 4 6 6 5 6 6 5 0 4 6 5 6 8
1 7 5 9 0 0 2 0 5 6 5 8 5 1 9 5 3 3 7 4 0 5 8 2 4
0 3 9 6 9 4 7 3 5 7 0 6 5 4 7 1 1 8 5 3 2 8 0 9 8
3 0 8 2 8 1 4 4 1 6 7 6 6 9 9 9 7 5 8 9 6 4 5 9 9
9 4 9 1 2 2 0 1 3 2 4 6 7 9 1 8 8 2 9 8 3 2 6 2 9
7 2 5 1 4 4 9 6 5 2 8 5 5 1 0 8 2 6 2 0 6 9 2 2 3
9 9 2 5 7 4 3 1 2 3 6 4 1 5 2 4 0 4 2 2 8 7 1 8 2
2 0 9 1 8 9 4 4 6 1 4 8 6 7 9 2 5 0 6 9 3 3 0 1 2
6 5 2 6 1 2 1 7 7 1 4 7 8 1 4 2 7 3 7 4 0 0 1 2 9
1 2 9 9 6 4 2 5 3 2 7 4 3 2 3 3 8 5 3 3 6 5 5 3 2
3 2 8 3 7 9 6 0 4 8 6 0 5 4 1 1 4 9 0 5 0 9 4 4 1
0 9 3 4 1 1 9 5 8 3 2 4 6 7 3 4 4 9 2 3 7 2 5 7 8
6 7 5 3 4 2 1 5 5 0 1 2 4 7 5 5 2 6 8 7 8 2 8 0 3
9 6 0 1 3 0 5 3 6 6 2 9 6 0 3 4 7 6 1 1 9 1 6 5 3
4 6 9 9 6 7 8 5 8 1 2 9 2 6 2 4 4 9 0 5 5 4 5 2 0
9 7 7 1 9 2 6 5 6 3 3 6 3 6 8 3 9 9 8 7 7 2 7 9 7
7 5 3 3 3 3 7 3 7 6 7 3 9 1 1 2 3 9 0 9 5 9 6 5 7
2 8 1 3 1 3 4 2 1 0 3 1 2 3 2 0 2 3 9 7 7 5 0 6 9
6 0 9 4 8 8 5 5 3 7 9 0 0 0 0 1 9 2 0 6 1 5 8 4 2
3 5 9 0 7 7 0 1 8 1 2 9 3 4 6 9 2 8 9 8 9 8 6 5 5
4 4 8 1 1 7 4 4 7 4 4 4 1 6 5 9 3 6 5 9 8 3 2 4 3
6 3 9 7 0 6 2 5 3 3 2 6 0 5 1 2 4 3 7 1 0 7 8 2 1
```

(Continued)

You may want to randomize more than ten items, so that you need to use two columns at a time. If you do this according to the instructions on the table, you will have to throw out most of the numbers because they are too large. There is a little trick, however, which allows you to randomize numbers from 10 to 50 without wasting either numbers or time.

Say you need to randomize 14 items. Divide 14 into each of the two-digit numbers you use and take the remainder as your result. For example, if using the first two columns, the first number is 82. Fourteen goes into 82 five times with a remainder of 12; it goes into the next number, 08, zero times with a remainder of 8; into 23 once with a remainder of 9, etc. Thus your first three random numbers are 12, 8, and 9.

The one thing you must be careful of when using this system is that every number between 1 and 14 has an equal chance of being selected. You make sure of this by using only those numbers that are even multiples of 14. Since 14 x 7 = 98, each of the numbers between 1 and 14 has seven different opportunities for being chosen from the numbers 1 to 98. But unless we discard the numbers 99 and 100 (let us consider the 00 combination as 100), variables 1 and 2 would each have eight chances of being chosen.

Let us try another example, the number 27. Divide 27 into 100. It goes three times with a remainder of 19. Only the numbers from 1 to 81 (3 x 27 = 81) should be used to randomize the 27 variables. This way each variable has exactly the same three chances of being chosen. The 19 numbers from 82 to 100 cannot be used since, if they were, the first 19 variables would each have an extra opportunity to be picked.

This type of plot placement is called **completely random** experimental design. It is the best method for randomizing treatments in experiments with animals or when you are working in a laboratory or greenhouse where growing conditions are quite uniform. It is the simplest of the random designs, but there are drawbacks to using it for field experiments.

Completely Random Plot Layout Showing
4 Treatments with 3 Replications

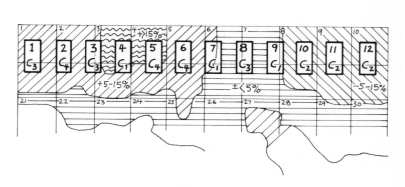

Figure 3-26

In looking at Figure 3-26, note that with a completely random placement of treatments, replications of some of the variables turn out to be bunched together. Since soil in adjacent plots tends to be similar, it turns out that all three of the replications of treatment C_2 are next to one another on the poorest soil. Over on the other side of the field, two plots of variety C_3 are on some of the best soil. So we can see that this completely random design is not really a fair way to compare the four treatments.

Also, 12 plots of 162 square feet each are quite a bit to care for. Perhaps on one day you cannot put in all your seed or do all the weeding. Arbitrarily deciding to do some weeding one day and the rest on the next cool day may bias your results by giving the plants in the weeded plots a head start.

The **randomized block** design works around these problems by grouping one of each of the treatments into a separate block and having as many blocks as there are replications. Thus each block is one complete replication of the experiment. We end up with the same 12 plots but now have a bit more control over their placement.

Other advantages are that differences in the soil or in weather conditions over the whole experimental area are less likely to be a factor within a single block. Several people can work together on the same experiment by having one person take care of one block while someone else takes care of another. If problems occur within one of the blocks, the whole replication can be dropped from the analysis without jeopardizing the validity of the entire experiment.

Let us now go back and lay out the four variety trial again, this time using three blocks of four treatments each (see Figure 3-27). The first replication will be in plots 1 to 4, the second block will be plots 5 to 8, and the third block, plots 9 to 12. Each replication is randomized separately.

> Let us use the block 2, 3 (second from the left, third from the top) from the Table of Random Permutations of 16. For the first replication only numbers 1 to 4 are used and the rest discarded. The plots are assigned as follows: 6, 15, 9, 5, 2 (treatment C_1); 16, 7, 13, 12, 1 (treatment C_2); 11, 14, 4 (treatment C_3); and 8, 10, 3 (treatment C_4). Use the numbers 5 to 8 from the next column (5, 9, 16, 4, 1, 6, 13, 8, 2, 3, 15, 7, 11, 10, 14, 12) for the second replication. C_1 is placed in plot 5, C_2 in plot 6, C_3 in plot 8, and C_4 in plot 7. For the third replication use the numbers 9 to 12 from the third column, assigning C_1 to plot 10, C_2 to plot 11, C_3 to plot 9, and C_4 to plot 12.

As you can see from Figure 3-27, with this design the treatments are more evenly dispersed over the experimental site. While there are still soil differences within the blocks, they are less than before. In addition, they can be dealt with under the auspices of "local control," a principle of experimentation that basically says that the worker on the job should use his or her head and make adjustments as long as they do not bias the results.

For example, three of the four plots of the third replication are on poor soil according to the results of the uniformity trials. To give greater validity to the comparison of the treatments within this block, all four of them should be on the same quality soil. The entire replication can be moved over to allow for this or, if the soil is considered too poor to

Randomized Block Design Showing 4 Treatments with 3 Replications

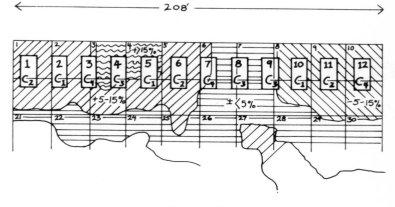

Figure 3-27

be worth experimenting on, the block could be moved to a different part of the field or to a different field. As you can see, the randomized block design allows for a great deal of flexibility. It works well for up to about 15 variables; with more, the blocks have usually gotten too large to be homogeneous.

Using the Randomized Block Design for Small Experiments

The randomized block design also works well when used for small-scale experiments comparing only two variables. With these, the randomizing can be done with a simple flip of a coin! The basic principles of the randomized block design are that the different treatments be grouped together in blocks, which are the most homogeneous units possible, and that there be several replications of these blocks. The replications all can be within one garden or farm field or they can be dispersed.

So if you and a group of fellow gardeners wish to try out a new variety or a new gardening technique, each of you can have one block of two plots in your own garden. Thus each of you will be caring for one replicate of the experiment and together you will have a statistically valid experiment laid out in a randomized block design.

Box 3-12: Estimating a Missing Value

It sometimes happens that after your experiment is well on its way, something goes wrong so that you cannot collect data from all of your plots. Maybe the neighborhood squirrels have decided to bury their winter stores in the soft garden soil of one of your plots and in so doing they uprooted most of the young plants. Since the resulting low yield has nothing to do with the experimental treatment, it is not valid to use these data in your analysis. But you can't just ignore this plot without dropping the entire block from the experiment. Instead of losing all that information, you can use a mathematical formula which has been designed to estimate the missing value from a randomized block experiment:

$$\frac{rB + tT - G}{(r-1)(t-1)} = \text{estimate of missing value}$$

where:
- r = the number of replicates
- B = the total value of observations from other treatments in the same block as the missing value
- t = the number of treatments
- T = the total value of the same treatment (as the missing value) from other blocks in the experiment
- G = grand total

For example, if you are experimenting with different amounts of organic nitrogen fertilizer on a spinach crop and are using five levels of treatment with three replications, your data may look like Figure 3-28.

Using Data from Randomized Block Experiment to Estimate Missing Value

treatment		replication	1	2	3	
1	no fertilizer		7	9	6	
2	5 lbs.		8	11	8	
3	10 lbs.		11	missing	10	
4	15 lbs.		12	14	13	
5	20 lbs.		13	13	12	
	totals (lbs./plot)		51	47	49	147

Using the formula to find an estimate of the missing value,

$$\frac{rB + tT - G}{(r-1)(t-1)}$$

$$\frac{3(47) + 5(21) - 147}{(3-1)(5-1)} =$$

$$\frac{141 + 105 - 147}{(2)(4)} =$$

$$\frac{246 - 147}{8} =$$

$$\frac{99}{8} = 12.4$$

Figure 3-28

Source: Yates 1933 (cited in Cochran and Cox 1957 and Cox 1958).

Another design to consider is the **Latin square** which randomizes the placement of variables in two directions to compensate for irregular soil quality (see Figure 3-29). Each treatment appears just once in each row and in each column; thus there are as many replicates as treatments. It is best suited for experiments with from four to eight treatments since with fewer than four replications, the results would be statistically questionable, while with more than eight the Latin square would be unwieldy.

The Latin square is not as flexible a design as the randomized block. Replications cannot be separated spatially or individually analyzed. If there is a problem with one of the treatments, such as missing data, it is more difficult to statistically compensate for the missing information with a Latin square than with a randomized block design.

However, it is the best layout for an experiment where all the replications are planned for a single garden or field and where soil quality variations are either unknown or very irregular.

Treatments can be assigned to plots either by rotation or by separately randomizing each row or column. If you have five treatments (A, B, C, D, E) and are assigning them by rotation, the variables in the first row would be in the order A-B-C-D-E, in the second row B-C-D-E-A, in the third row C-D-E-A-B, and so on, as shown in the illustration.

If you prefer to place the treatments randomly rather than by rotation, it would probably be easier to pull numbers from a hat rather than to use a random number table since you are dealing with a few variables. Write the symbol for each treatment on separate slips of paper and mix them up well. The treatment written on the slip of paper chosen first goes into the first plot, the next into the second, and so on. Just be careful that you do not end up with the same treatment appearing more than once in any one of the columns or rows.

As you may have noticed from Figure 3-29, the Latin square does not actually have to be square.

Lastly, you should be aware of the **split-plot design**, which is a modification of either the randomized block or Latin square designs. It is used exclusively for factorial experiments. Factorial experiments can be laid out using the regular randomized block or Latin square designs, but sometimes it is more efficient to use a split-plot.

Such would be the case if you were doing an experiment comparing the efficiency of several different methods of watering: (1) laying a soak hose along the row; (2) attaching a sprinkler to your garden hose; and (3) watering from a

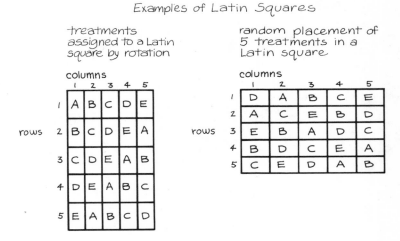

Figure 3-29

pail just around the base of your plants. If you wanted to see how the different watering methods worked in mulched and unmulched plots, this would then be a factorial experiment because you would be working with two factors simultaneously.

You could randomize the placement of all six plots, but this would require moving the soak hose and the sprinkler attachment back and forth between the plots where their use was called for. The experiment would be easier to handle if there were three large plots, one for each of the watering systems. Each of these would be subdivided into two subplots, one of which would be mulched and the other would not. These two ways of handling a factorial experiment are illustrated in Figure 3-30.

The designs which we have described are not the only ones available, but are the more basic ones which you would most likely use. If you are planning a very complex experiment and are interested in other designs (and have the statistical background to analyze the results), you can find elaborate discussions in Cochran and Cox 1957, Cox 1958, Fisher and Yates 1974, Hopp 1954, Jeffers 1960, LeClerg, Leonard, and Clark 1962, Little and Hills 1975,

Ways of Handling a Factorial Experiment

Using a randomized block design for a factorial experiment

Using a split-plot modification of the randomized block design

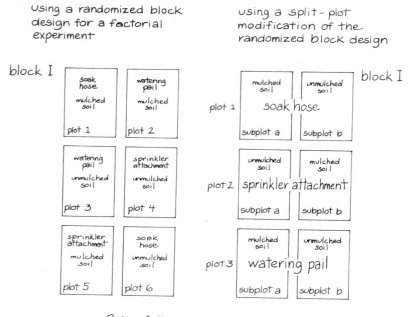

block I

soak hose	watering pail
mulched soil	mulched soil
plot 1	plot 2

watering pail	sprinkler attachment
unmulched soil	unmulched soil
plot 3	plot 4

sprinkler attachment	soak hose
mulched soil	unmulched soil
plot 5	plot 6

plot 1 — soak hose
| mulched soil | unmulched soil |
| subplot a | subplot b |

plot 2 — sprinkler attachment
| unmulched soil | mulched soil |
| subplot a | subplot b |

plot 3 — watering pail
| mulched soil | unmulched soil |
| subplot a | subplot b |

block I

Both of these examples show just one replication of the experiment.

Figure 3-30

Patterson 1939, Pettygrove 1971 (1976), Snedecor and Cochran 1967, and Townsend 1973.

Note

1. That is why researchers are paying increasingly more attention to testing the nutrient status of the *plant*, rather than the soil. Though this is still an inexact science, potentially it is of as much value as soil testing because it shows how well the plant itself is utilizing the nutrients. While a soil test may indicate a respectable level of a certain nutrient, that does not insure that the plant is reaping the benefits. Drought, pH level, and the binding of certain

chemicals can all play a part in preventing full utilization of soil nutrients.

Tissue analysis of plants can be done in a chemistry laboratory. However, if the lab is not specifically set up to do this type of work, the analysis can become quite costly. Check the Yellow Pages of your telephone directory under "Chemists—Analytical and Consulting" to see if any local laboratories are willing and able to do nutrient analyses and what the costs would be. Laboratories at some of the land grant colleges are equipped to do this work for the public at a nominal fee.

Urbana Laboratories sells an inexpensive kit with reagents to test for nitrogen, phosphorus, and potassium. To use the kit you squeeze sap from a plant onto a specially treated blotting paper and add the reagent. Depending on the nutrient level (high, medium, low), the mixture will turn a predictable color. This gives an indication of nutrient status, but obviously it is not a precise measure.

One of the problems with plant-nutrient analysis is that healthy plants of the same type growing in the same place may still respond differently to the chemical tests. It is not yet known how variable plants are and, therefore, how big a sample is needed to represent their diversity. Also, depending on the time of the year and on the particular part of the plant being sampled, different amounts of the nutrient will be found. These differences reflect the metabolic processes occurring at that time and in that place.

It is considered best to use a mature, undamaged leaf from just below the growing tip on the main stem and to sample at a time when the plant is not under moisture or temperature stress. Sampling is best done just before the reproductive stage, since once flowering and fruiting begin, the vegetative portion of the plant undergoes changes. More research must be done to figure out how plant needs correlate with test results at different times.

Nutrient status can also be assessed by looking at plant leaves and general growth patterns for indications of deficiencies. A lack of nitrogen, for example, shows up as a pale green to yellow color on older growth. Most introductory soils textbooks contain brief sections on these nutrient indicators. The book *Hunger Signs in Crops* (Sprague 1964) goes into great detail for a variety of plants.

For more information on the subject of testing for plant nutrients, see Krantz, Nelson, and Burkhart 1948, and Walsh and Beaton 1973.

4

Carrying Out the Experiment

LAYING OUT PLOTS

Designs can look beautiful on paper but laying them out in
the field so that they are the intended size and shape can be
tricky. By putting into practical application a theorem you
probably learned in basic geometry, you will, however, be
able to lay out a rectangle that is truly rectangular.

Do you remember Pythagoras, the ancient Greek
philosopher? He is credited with discovering that if you add
the squares of the two shorter sides of a right triangle, the
sum equals the square of the diagonal. This idea is written
with the formula $a^2 + b^2 = c^2$. Once the lengths of the three
sides of a right triangle have been computed, it follows that
any time a triangle is drawn with sides of these lengths or in
this ratio it will have a 90° angle. We can apply this information in laying out the right angles of our rectangular plots.

To make the jump from theory to practice, we will use
a triangle with sides in a 3:4:5 ratio as shown in Figure 4-1.

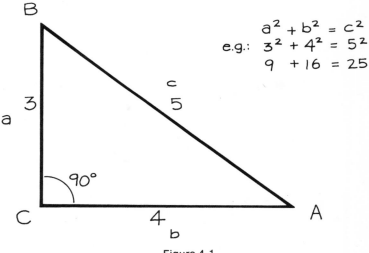

Right Triangle with Sides
in a 3:4:5 Ratio

$$a^2 + b^2 = c^2$$
$$e.g.: \quad 3^2 + 4^2 = 5^2$$
$$9 + 16 = 25$$

Figure 4-1

We choose this ratio since it is easiest to work with whole numbers. Find the multiple of the 3:4 ratio which comes closest to the dimensions of your plot. For example, a randomized block 10 feet x 18 feet would use a triangle with dimensions of 15 feet x 20 feet x 25 feet.

With a rope knotted or otherwise marked at 15 feet, 20 feet, and 25 feet, first mark off the 20-foot baseline by putting in a stake at each end. Then, standing at point "C," stretch out the rope approximately perpendicular to the baseline and, 15 feet from point "C," scratch out an arc in the soil by swinging the rope. Starting from point "A," stretch out the rope 25 feet and draw another arc, intercepting the first. This point of interception is called "B" and is the third point of the right triangle. Now you can be certain that the two sides of the triangle are exactly perpendicular and you can measure off the precise dimensions of your plot.

This precision is necessary if you plan to compare

Using a Right Triangle to Determine Exact Dimensions of a Garden Plot

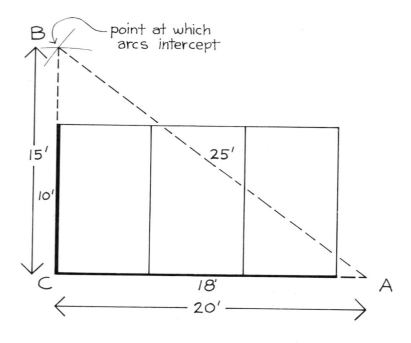

Figure 4-2

yields from plots that are supposed to be of equal size or if you are multiplying the yield of a small plot to find a projected yield per acre. A small measurement error in a small plot multiplies out to a large error per acre.

SPACING BETWEEN PLANTS

When, on the other hand, you are measuring yield per plant, precise spacing between *plants* becomes important so that no plant has an advantage or disadvantage in the competition for sun, moisture, nutrients, and space. Use a tape measure or a string marked off at the appropriate intervals to guide your placement of seeds.

Except when doing germination tests, it is best to over-plant and then thin to the desired density. Then you are certain to have a plant at each designated interval. Another possibility is to raise extra plants for transplanting in case some of the originals do not survive.

HOW MANY PLOTS ARE NEEDED?

Before you even get to the point of laying out plots or putting in seed, you must determine how many plots are needed to accommodate all the treatments you plan with sufficient replication. A controlled experiment requires at least two different treatments for comparative purposes.

In its simplest form this experiment can be a variety trial where the performance of a new variety is tested against an old standby. In a garden, this would call for several pairs of equal-sized plots, with one of the plots in each pair planted in the new variety and one in the familiar old variety. Or you could have one pair of plots in your garden and the other pairs in neighbors' gardens, in that way replicating the experiment.

Often on farms the standard crop is planted as usual over most of the field with a small area set aside for the new variety. However, it is important that this new variety does not get relegated to some agricultural outpost or to a single row strip at the edge of the larger field, but that it and the main crop are planted on land of comparable quality. The plots should be wide enough to provide for the border effect and, as with any other experiment, there should be several replicates (see Figure 4-3).

Areas equal in size to the new plots must be designated as sampling areas for the main crop *before* planting proceeds. This eliminates the personal bias involved if sampling areas are chosen at harvesttime. Then, if you really wanted the new variety to "win," your eye might subconsciously seek out the more barren spots in the larger field for comparison with the test plots.

95

Plot Layout for a Variety Trial

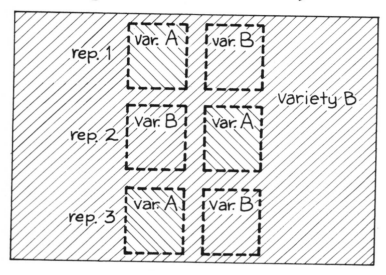

Figure 4-3

Single-factor experiments can also be done with more than two different treatments. When they are, the results generally convey more information than they do with a simple two-variable project. Say, for example, you want to test the benefits of mulching cucumbers. So you set up a project to measure soil temperature and growth rates and yields of plants growing in bare soil vs. those growing under a clear plastic mulch. If your results are typical, they will show a higher yield from mulched plants.

But why is that? Mulches are credited with maintaining more even soil moisture conditions, with raising soil temperature early in the season and moderating it later on, and with preventing weed growth. To find out which of these factors were important in raising your yields, you might try an experiment comparing different types of mulches.

Using cucumbers grown on bare soil as your control, have a plot for plants grown with a black plastic mulch. This mulch restricts weed growth and also may keep soil temperatures lower during the early part of the season. Have another plot using a clear plastic mulch. This mulch permits some weed growth but accounts for a significant increase in soil temperatures early in the season, while in the mid-season heat, soil beneath the mulch is usually cooler than bare soil. Finally, have a plot where the clear plastic is removed one and a half weeks after planting. This results in the most consistently high soil temperatures throughout the season.

If your results are similar to those of two Finnish scientists (Pessala and Hardh 1977), you will find that the plots with clear plastic mulch removed after one and a half weeks had the highest yields, while the yields from plots with dark mulch did not differ significantly from those with only bare soil. Now you can conclude not only that some types of mulch help in producing higher yields, but that for growing cucumbers in cold climates, the ability of mulch to raise soil temperatures is more important than its ability to suppress weed growth. This new information can guide your decisions on when to use mulch and which factors to look for in choosing a mulch.

Either a randomized block or a Latin square design would work well for this experiment since it has four treatments. It is good to get into the habit of listing the proposed treatments along with abbreviations for them before randomizing the placement of plots (see Figure 4-4). By setting this information down on paper, you can see more clearly if

Listing Proposed Treatments for a Simple Experiment

factor	mulching treatments	abbreviation
variables	bare soil black plastic used all season clear plastic removed at 1½ weeks clear plastic used all season	b s c p c p 1½ b p
number	4	

Figure 4-4

Listing Proposed Treatments for a Factorial Experiment

factors	variety	interplanting density	treatments	
variables	Spartan Early (SE) Waltham (W)	no onions (NO) broccoli : onions 1:1 (1:1) broccoli : onions 1:2 (1:2) broccoli : onions 1:5 (1:5) no broccoli, just onions (NB)	SE NO SE 1:1 SE 1:2 SE 1:5 NB W NO W 1:1 W 1:2 W 1:5	
number	2 x	5	= 10 -1 9	

Spartan Early (SE) and Waltham (W) varieties of broccoli are each planted alone and in 3 different proportions with onions. Only 1 plot is needed with onions alone. This gives a total of 9 plots in each replication.

Figure 4-5

the plans meet your goals and if the variety and range of treatments you envision are actually the ones you are carrying out.

This practice will serve you well should you move on to more complicated factorial experiments. These simultaneously compare different treatments on two or more factors. To figure the number of plots needed, list each factor and each of the variables for that factor in the same way as is done in Figure 4-4. Then multiply the number of variables for one factor by the number of variables for each of the others. Give each of the variables a symbol so that when you multiply, you also get a unique symbolic configuration which then becomes the "code name" for that treatment.

The example shown in Figure 4-5 is from an experiment measuring insect damage on two varieties of broccoli planted alone or interplanted with onions in different ratios. Since it is not necessary to have two plots with onions planted alone, one treatment is subtracted from the sum total.

Factorial experiments can involve more than two factors. It's only fair to warn you, however, that the analysis of the results then becomes quite complex.

LABELING

The "code names" given to the treatments can be used any time you want to identify the treatment: place them on stakes showing what is being grown in which plot and for any samples taken from the plots. When you need to be able to identify individual plants, use 4-inch wooden or plastic pot markers—available at farm and garden supply stores or biological supply houses. Get the type with precut holes, or drill the holes yourself, put a wire or string through the hole, and tie it loosely around the plant. These are more visible and safer than lots of little stakes poking up from the ground all over your plot.

Write the treatment code on one side and the plant number on the other with indelible marker or grease pencil. When you are dealing with more than one replication, add

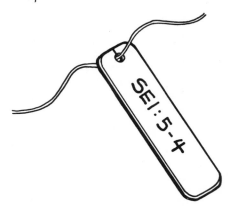

Label to Identify a Plant
Sample in a Garden Plot

Figure 4-6

A Permanent Label to Identify a Sample in a Collection

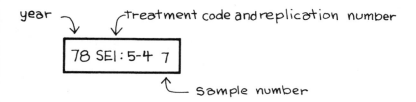

Figure 4-7

a replication number to the treatment code. For example, labels identifying samples of Spartan Early broccoli grown in a ratio of 1 broccoli plant to 5 onion plants in the fourth replication of the experiment would look like Figure 4-6.

Labels for plant and insect samples belong inside the collection bag or jar rather than taped onto the outside where they may fall off. Cut strips of white paper approximately 1½ inch x ½ inch for your labels. Use a good-quality paper with a high cloth content so it will not disintegrate if kept in a jar of alcohol with some insects or inside a plastic bag with damp plants. Temporary labels can be written in pencil, but if you want them to remain legible for a long period of time, it is best to write in black India ink. The information on the label should include the year (since some experiments are repeated over several seasons), the treatment code, the replication number, and the sample number (see Figure 4-7).

RECORD KEEPING

This information is keyed into your notebook, which should have a page set aside for the data collected from each plot. Here you record the date of collection, an identifying description of the sample, and other pertinent data such as the weight or leaf surface area (see Figure 4-8).

There are two maxims of scientific record keeping:

1. Do not write anything on a scrap of paper.

2. Do not assume you will remember something that is not written down.

Data and observations from scientific experiments are, in fact, supposed to be recorded in ink in bound notebooks

Page from a Notebook

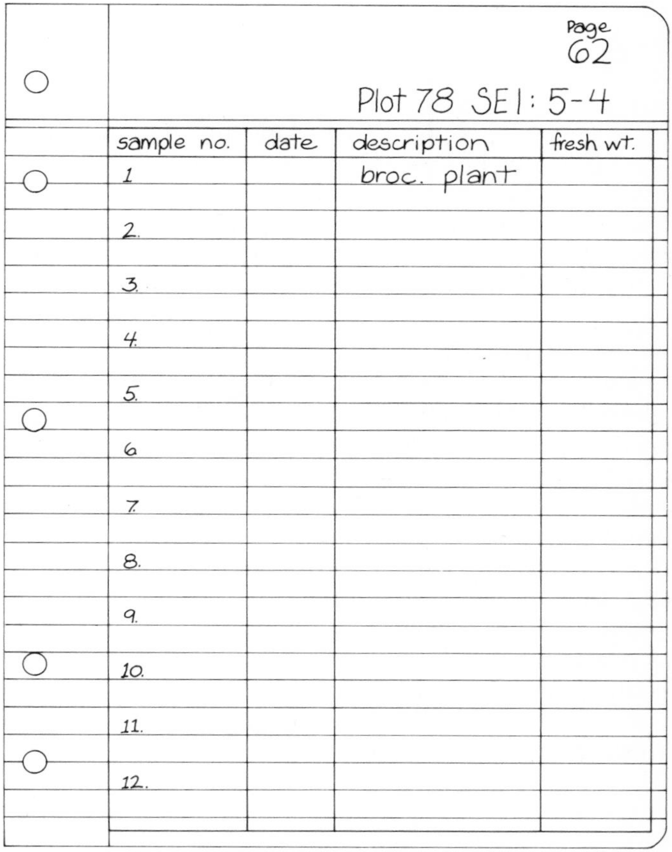

	sample no.	date	description	fresh wt.	
				Page 62	
○			Plot 78 SE1: 5-4		
○	1		broc. plant		
	2.				
	3.				
	4.				
	5.				
○	6				
	7.				
	8.				
	9.				
○	10.				
	11.				
○	12.				

Figure 4-8

to verify the integrity of the data collection. Your notebook should have a section for field notes and a section for data. Also include a map showing plot layout in case, as is very likely, something should happen to some of the identifying stakes placed in the field.

CARRYING OUT THE EXPERIMENT

While the experiment is still in the planning stages, try to determine what care and maintenance the plots will need and what information must be collected to adequately test your hypothesis. You may want to run through a small pilot project first to give you a sense of how the experimental work proceeds before you embark on a full-scale venture.

If several people are working together on a project, each operation or task should be carried out by the same person on all the treatments since people's different styles of working can affect experimental results. It would introduce an experimental error if one person did the planting for treatments A and B while another person who, perhaps, planted the seeds a little deeper took on that task for treatments C and D.

Remember that your data is only as valid as the work that goes into the experiment so you must be sure to regularly and uniformly carry out maintenance chores and observations. It follows that your conclusions also are only as valid as the data from which they are drawn. Thus if your ideas are too ambitious for your time schedule, assume that one or the other is eventually going to fall through, and make the necessary alterations in your plans with forethought.

A grandiose scheme in the month of May that proves too time-consuming or complicated by mid-July will have taught you less than a simple plan regularly followed through the season.

PART II

EXPERIMENTS AND RESEARCH PROJECTS

So far, you've learned methods for researching and experimenting which, if followed, will result in valid scientific data from your tests. Now you may want to try out some of these techniques by carrying out a research project or doing an experiment yourself.

You may already have plenty of ideas for experiments after reading the first part of this book. This section suggests more, first by looking at some scientific research and then outlining ways that you can replicate or expand upon it. Consider these four chapters a place to *start;* allow yourself time to explore your own ideas, pursue other avenues of inquiry, and follow up on your observations. A raging curiosity is an essential for a good researcher.

5

Presowing Seed Treatments

Life begins with the seed. Thus, it is fitting that our first experiments involve testing various seed treatments, especially since they can be conducted indoors—at least in part—during that restless pregardening season.

Some very fascinating work has been done to test the effects of exposing seeds to controlled electrostatic and magnetic fields. In fact, the effects of electrostatic and magnetic fields on *all* biological processes are being acknowledged in more and more areas. Honeybees lose their orientation and horses rear up and go out of control around high-tension power lines. Experiments have shown that a positive electrical field slows the development of *Nepytia* pupae (a type of geometrid moth) and significantly decreases the percentage of germination of lettuce seed. On the other hand, experimental results have repeatedly shown increased germination rates and yields when seeds are exposed to a magnetic field, especially when the embryo points to magnetic north.

Those with an affinity for the world of electricity and magnetism might use some of the experiments in the following sources as an inspiration or a prototype: Barnothy 1964; Lebedev et al. 1975; Novitsky and Tikhomir 1977; Pittman 1963, 1965, 1967, 1977; Sidaway 1966; Strekova et al. 1965; and Tarakanova et al. 1965.

Less esoteric than the experiments with electrostatic and magnetic fields, also with less conclusive results, are experiments involving the soaking of seeds in water before planting to increase germination and yield. One theory is that soaking increases the seeds' ability to withstand conditions of drought and cold.

Russian workers, experimenting with "hardening" seed by alternating periods of wetting and drying, found that plants from the hardened seed had increased yields.[1] They attributed this to modifications in the cytoplasm of hardened seed which enabled them to better withstand drought. English scientists working with carrot seed substantiated these results, but attributed the increased yields to the three-to four-day head start which the treated seed had as a result of their more rapid germination.

Not all of the results have been so positive; a number of experimenters found either no advantage at all or that seed was destroyed by soaking, perhaps due to internal "explosions" of cell walls with the rapid uptake of water.

How would you like to add your own two cents to this conflicting maze of experimental results? Obviously there are no foregone conclusions. Each different variety of seed tested can provide new information. Even seed of the same variety grown in different localities can react differently.[2] (For further reading see Berrie and Drennan 1971; Buxton et al. 1977; Chippingdale 1933, 1934; Genkel et al. 1964; Gray and Steckel 1977; and Polya 1961.)

The experimental procedures that follow are adapted in part from an article entitled "Some Effects of 'Hardening' Carrot Seed" (Austin et al. 1969). Exact details, such as those concerning the size of the plot and the planting density, will differ with the seed you decide to test. Your experiment can either be done very simply, using one variety of seed and one method of seed hardening or you can make matters more complex by using different varieties of seed, different water : seed ratios, or by going through more than one cycle to harden the seeds. These procedures will increase the amount of information conveyed by your results, but will also make them more difficult to analyze.

HARDENING SEED

Hardening seed involves soaking and then drying it. You can experiment with different ratios of water to seed weight to find the optimum for the presowing treatment. Use 1-ounce packets of seed so it will be easy to measure the appropriate amounts of water for the various ratios. You will need one packet for a control group and one for each of the

Preparing Seeds for Germination by Subjecting to Different Numbers of Hardening Cycles

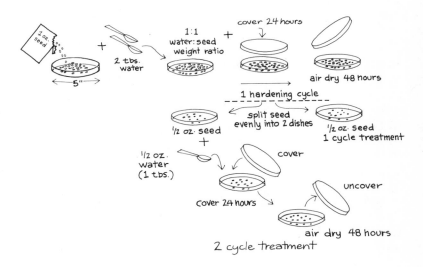

Figure 5-1

weight ratios tested. If you are working with large, heavy seed like peas, beans, or corn, you will need to use multiples of the 1-ounce packet.

Since 1 ounce of water is 2 tablespoons or 6 teaspoons, you need 2 *teaspoons* of water for a 1:3 weight ratio, 4 for a 2:3 ratio, and 6 for a 1:1 ratio, etc.

Put the contents of each seed packet into separate, flat-bottomed containers about 5 inches in diameter (see Figure 5-1). Plastic freezer containers work well as do shallow dishes which can be covered with cellophane or plastic. Sprinkle the measured amount of water into each dish and label it with the sample number, then cover it. After 24 hours, remove the cover and let the seeds air dry for 48 hours.[3] This is one hardening cycle. You can repeat this process with part of the treated seed, using proportionally less water. Then you will be able to compare seeds which have been subjected to different numbers of hardening cycles.

GERMINATION TEST

For the germination test shown in Figure 5-2, use shallow containers such as saucers or petri dishes, which can be purchased from a biological supply house. Place a piece of filter paper, folded paper towel, or cotton cloth on the dish and keep it moist throughout the experiment. Use 50 seeds per sample, spreading them evenly in a single layer on the toweling. While the control seeds do not go through any soaking treatment, they too are spread on moist paper in a shallow dish and otherwise treated in the same manner as the hardened seed.

Check each dish frequently to make sure it is still moist and record the number of normal, healthy seedlings daily or on alternate days. The dishes should be kept in a warm, well-lighted place, arranged in a completely random pattern, as described in Chapter 3.

You could use a chart like the one shown to record your data. To see if there is a significant difference in the percentage of germination of treated vs. control seeds, see

Germination Experiment

This is sample replicate #1 of the treatment with a 2:3 water: seed weight ratio and 3 hardening cycles.

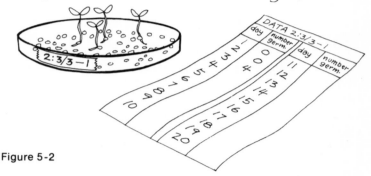

Figure 5-2

Chapter 9, Box 9-4, or use the table of "Intervals of Success" which is shown and explained in Chapter 9, Box 9-6.

Germination tests can also be done to determine the viability of seeds—seeds that you have collected yourself, perhaps, or seeds that you have saved for a number of years. Growing plants for their seeds, selecting the plants which have seed worth saving, hand pollinating to insure specific plant characteristics, and plant breeding are all fertile areas for experimentation by the backyard researcher. There are a number of excellent books that cover the subject in great detail. If you're interested in pursuing this area further, consult some of the following references: *Agricultural and Horticultural Seeds* 1961; Allard 1960; *Breeding Plants for Home and Garden* 1974; Bubel 1978; Hayes and Immer 1942; Johnston 1976; Miller 1977; Roberts 1972; Whyte 1958; and Yearbooks of Agriculture 1936, 1961.

FIELD TESTS

Germination percentages are usually lower outdoors due to climate and soil pathogens. Thus, to get an accurate sense of actual germination rates, the germination tests should be repeated under field conditions. The results of your indoor experimentation can be used, however, to simplify the fieldwork. You may have discovered after analyzing your data that the various water:seed ratios and number of hardening cycles either had no effect on germination rates or that one of them produced significantly better results than the others. In either case you can choose one of the treatments for your future work rather than using all six, and compare that one with the nontreated control. The experiment can be laid out using a randomized block design as shown in Figure 5-3.

Use 50 seeds per plot. The size of your plot will depend on the planting density recommended for the crop you are experimenting with. A plot of carrots planted every 3 inches in three rows 1 foot apart would be about 3 feet by 4 feet, while a plot of corn planted every 8 inches in three rows 2½ feet apart would be closer to 5 feet by 10 feet.

For your field experiments you may want to test other factors such as planting both the treatment and the control on several different dates and/or varying the amount that they are watered during the season. The purpose of using different planting dates is to see how climatic conditions, particularly cold and dryness, relate to the effectiveness of the hardening treatments.

Using Randomized Block Design for Plot Layout in Field Experiments

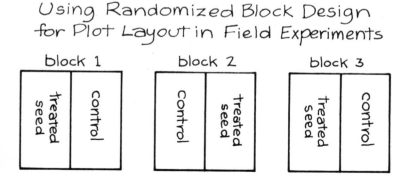

Figure 5-3

Record of Yield Data

treatment : control planted April 25, no watering
plot numbers : rep. 1-4, rep. 2-7, rep. 3-12
harvest date : Sept. 30

sample units	weight of carrot (oz.)			treatment total:	
	replications				
	1	2	3		
1					
2					
3					
4					
5					
6					
7					
8					
9					
10					
total yield				treatment total:	
mean yield				treatment mean :	treatment range :

Figure 5-4

Once you have collected data on the germination rate and evaluated that, you can let the plants grow and at the end of the season compare plot yields. For plots with just three rows, use only the plants in the center row for your sample (remember the "border effect!"). With plots of more than three rows, you can use one of the sampling methods discussed in Chapter 9 to choose which plants are to be measured. A chart like the one shown in Figure 5-4 can be used to collect yield data. This format can be used for many other types of experiments as well.

To find the total yield per plot, add the weights of the yields of each of your ten (or more) sample units. If you want to know the average weight per plant, divide this total by the number of sampling units. To find the average (mean) weight for the treatment, add the totals from the three replications and divide by 30. The range is the difference between the largest and the smallest of the 30 values. We discuss the evaluation of yield data in Chapter 9.

Above and beyond calculating which treatment gives

the best germination rate and yield, you have to decide if the seed-hardening process (or any other treatment, for that matter) was worth the effort. We talk about that too when discussing the evaluation of the experiment.

Notes

1. Genkel et al. 1964 (cited in Austin et al. 1969) found 10% increase in yield for treated wheat seed, 26% increase for corn, 10% for sugar beets, 7% for red beets, 18% for carrots, and 60% for tomatoes.

2. Seed used in the experiment on hardening of carrot seed probably came from the western United States where humidity is low during seed harvest. The authors hypothesize that the seed embryos never develop fully due to premature dehydration and that the soaking treatment belatedly gives them the chance to do so. This is substantiated by measurements of the embryos of treated and control seeds, showing larger embryos in the soaked seeds.

3. If all of the water has not been absorbed, measure the excess, and pour it off. Record the adjustment which you have made in the water:seed ratio.

6

Energetics

How much energy do you put into those gardening projects of yours? Or maybe you would rather not quantify this lovely, leisurely part of your life. But before you turn the page—have you ever thought about comparing the amount of energy it takes to create food with the amount of energy the food itself provides? Would you be surprised to find out that, when processing is included, industrial agricultural systems often get *less* energy from the edible portion of crops than was expended in producing the crop?

We have only been able to afford to continue eating due to the relatively low cost of fossil fuels, which represent a lot of caloric energy. Human labor, with its far lower caloric cost, is however, more expensive in monetary terms. In this age of the unstable dollar and questioning values of work done by machines vs. that done by hand, it is enlightening and refreshing to put all energy inputs into the same terms—whether they be the Btu, joule, or kilocalorie.

As Amory Lovins points out in *World Energy Strategies* (1975), "The energy in one U.S. gallon of oil is equivalent to one-and-a-half weeks of a fine diet of 3,000 food calories per day (more than most of the world's people get). The gallon lasts less than ten minutes in a fast car. A Concorde SST consumes it in about a tenth of a second. Millenia were consumed in putting the gallon together."

Several published studies have compared the energy and economic costs of food production in different agricultural systems. By using some of the conversion factors from these sources, you can do similar experiments with your own food-producing system. The results will help you to put your gardening efforts into perspective.

You can compare the amount of energy needed to raise different crops. If space is a problem in your garden, you can use this information to help decide which vegetables are most efficiently grown at home and which you might do better to purchase elsewhere. The amount of energy used to care for a particular crop in several different ways also can be compared. Then you can see if extra effort in watering, fertilizing, or cultivating is justified by an increased yield. And you can compare the amount of human energy needed to care for a garden with the amount of energy required to operate a Rototiller and other small machines.

All of these comparisons are made by looking at the ratio of food energy to energy inputs. The higher the ratio, the more efficient the system. This type of evaluation is valid when applied to the smaller scale of the backyard gardener using primarily human labor as well as for the larger scale of the commercial, mechanized farm. In either case, the energy value of a crop (also known as the "digestible energy") is calculated by multiplying the yield for a given area by the energy value per pound (see Table 6-1):

Pounds Produced in 1 Square Yard × Calories per Pound

For example, if ¾ pound of dry beans is produced in 1 square yard, then:

0.75 pounds/square yard × 1,542 calories/pound

= 1156.5 calories/square yard of dry beans.

(Continued on page 123)

Table 6-1—Energy Value in Edible Portion of 1 Pound of Food

Food and Description (refuse noted in parentheses)	Refuse %	Food Energy cal./lb.	Protein g./lb.
Amaranth, raw (tough stems, rootlets)	37	103	10.0
Apples, freshly harvested (core, stem)	8	234	0.8
Apricots, raw (12/lb.) (pits)	6	217	4.3
Asparagus, raw spears (butt ends)	44	66	6.4
Barley, pearled, pot or Scotch	0	1,579	43.5
Beans, black, brown and Bayo, raw	0	1,538	101.2
lima, immature seeds in pod, raw (pods)	60	223	15.2
Beans, mung, raw, mature dry seeds	0	1,542	109.8
pinto, calico and red Mexican, raw	0	1,583	103.9
red, raw	0	1,556	102.1
snap, green, raw (ends, strings, trimmings)	12	128	7.6
snap, yellow or wax, raw (ends, strings, trimmings)	12	108	6.8
white, raw	0	1,542	101.2
Beets, common, red, raw with tops (tops and parings)	60	78	2.9
without tops (parings)	30	137	5.1
Beet greens, common, raw (stems, bruises and tough leaves)	44	61	5.6
Blackberries, including boysenberries, dewberries and youngberries, raw (caps and damaged parts)	5	250	5.2

Table 6-1 (continued)

Food and Description (refuse noted in parentheses)	Refuse %	Food Energy cal./lb.	Protein g./lb.
Blueberries, raw (stems, soft or withered berries)	8	259	2.9
Breadfruit, raw (skin, stems, core)	23	360	5.9
Broad beans, also called fava beans, raw, immature seeds in pods (pods)	66	162	13.0
mature seeds, dry	0	1,533	113.9
Broccoli, raw, spears, un-trimmed (large leaves, tough stalks)	39	89	10.0
Brussels sprouts, raw (trimmings)	8	188	20.4
Buckwheat, whole grain	0	1,520	53.1
Cabbage, Chinese, compact heading type, raw (root base, tough wilted outer leaves)	12	56	4.8
common varieties, raw, untrimmed (outer leaves, core)	10	98	5.3
pakchoi, nonheading green leaf type, raw (root base and dam-aged leaves)	20	58	5.8
Carrots, raw, with full tops (tops, scrapings)	41	112	2.9
Cauliflower, raw, untrimmed (jacket and inner leaves, main stalk, base and core)	61	48	4.8
Celeriac, root, raw (parings)	14	156	7.0
Celery, raw (leaves, root ends, trimmings)	25	58	3.1

Table 6-1 (continued)

Food and Description (refuse noted in parentheses)	Refuse %	Food Energy cal./lb.	Protein g./lb.
Chard, Swiss, raw (tough stem ends and damaged leaves)	8	104	10.0
Cherries, raw, sour, red (pits)	8	242	5.0
sweet (pits and stems)	10	286	5.3
Chestnuts, fresh, in shell (shells)	19	713	10.7
Chick-peas or garbanzos, mature seeds, dry, raw	0	1,633	93.0
Chicory, witloof also called French or Belgian endive, raw, blanched (root base, core)	11	66	4.0
Chives, raw	0	127	8.2
Collards, raw, leaves including stems	0	181	16.3
Corn, field, whole grain, raw	0	1,579	40.4
sweet, with husk (husk, silk, cob, trimmings)	64	157	5.7
Cowpeas, including black-eyed peas, immature seeds, raw in pods (pods)	45	317	22.5
mature seeds, dry	0	1,556	103.4
Crabapples, raw (cores, stems)	8*	284	1.7
Cranberries, raw (stems, damaged berries)	4	200	1.7
Cress, garden, raw (stems, crowns, spoiled leaves)	29	103	8.4
Cucumbers, raw, whole (ends, bruised spots)	5	65	3.9
Dandelion greens, raw, fully trimmed	0	204	12.2

*These numbers indicate approximate percents.

Table 6-1 (continued)

Food and Description (refuse noted in parentheses)	Refuse %	Food Energy cal./lb.	Protein g./lb.
Dock, curly or narrow leaf, broadleaf, and sheep sorrel, raw (stem)	30	89	6.7
Eggplant, raw (ends, parings, trimmings)	19	92	4.4
Elderberries, raw (stems)	6	307	11.1
Endive, curly endive and escarole, raw (ends)	12	80	6.8
Filberts, hazelnuts, in shell (shells)	54	1,323	26.3
Garlic, cloves, raw (skins)	12	547	24.8
Grapes, raw, American type (slip skin) (stems, seeds, skins)	37	197	3.7
European type (adherent skin) (stems, seeds, shriveled)	11	270	2.4
Hickory nuts, in shell (shells)	65	1,068	21.0
Honey, strained or extracted	0	1,379	1.4
Hyacinth beans, raw, young pods (ends, strings, trim)	12	140	11.2
mature seeds, dry	0	1,533	100.7
Jackfruit, raw (seeds, skin)	72	124	1.7
Kale, raw, leaves and stems (stem ends, tough stems, tough midribs)	26	128	14.1
Kohlrabi, raw, with leaves (leaves with stems, parings)	54	61	4.2
Lamb's-quarters, raw, fully trimmed	0	195	19.1

Table 6-1 (continued)

Food and Description (refuse noted in parentheses)	Refuse %	Food Energy cal./lb.	Protein g./lb.
Leeks, bulb and lower leaf portion, raw (tops and rootlets)	48	123	5.2
Lentils, mature seeds, dry, raw	0	1,542	112.0
Lettuce, raw, butterhead varieties (outer leaves and core)	26	47	4.0
cos or romaine (outer leaves, core, trim)	36	52	3.8
looseleaf	36	52	3.8
Millet, proso, broomcorn, hog millet, whole grain (stem ends)	0	1,483	44.9
Mushrooms, *Agaricus campestris*, cultivated commercial, raw	3	123	11.9
other edible species, raw (mainly stem ends)	3	154	8.4
Muskmelons, raw, cantaloupes (rind, cavity contents)	50	68	1.6
Mustard greens, raw (coarse leaves, stems)	30	98	9.5
Nectarines, raw (pits)	8	267	2.5
New Zealand spinach, raw	0	86	10.0
Oats, rolled	0	1,769	64.4
Okra, raw (stem ends, tips)	14	140	9.4
Onions, mature, dry, raw (skin ends)	9	157	6.2
young, green, bunching varieties, raw bulb and entire top used (rootlet)	4	157	6.5

Table 6-1 (continued)

Food and Description (refuse noted in parentheses)	Refuse %	Food Energy cal./lb.	Protein g./lb.
Papaws, common, North American type, raw (rind, seeds)	25	289	17.7
Papayas, raw (skin, seeds)	33	119	1.8
Parsley, raw	0	200	16.3
Parsnips, raw (parings)	15	293	6.6
Peaches, raw, peeled (thin skins, pits)	13	150	2.4
Peanuts, raw, in shell (shells)	27	1,868	86.1
Pears, raw (stem and core)	9	252	2.9
Peas, edible podded, raw (tips, strings)	5	228	14.7
green, immature, raw, in pods (pods)	62	145	10.9
mature seeds, dry, raw, whole	0	1,542	109.3
Pecans, in shell (shells)	47	1,652	22.1
Peppers, hot chili, green, raw (stem ends, seeds, core)	27*	123	4.3
hot chili, mature, red, pods with seeds (stem ends)	4	405	16.1
sweet, garden variety, immature green, raw, (stem ends, seeds, core)	18	82	4.5
mature, red, raw (stem ends, seeds, core)	20	112	5.1
Plums (pits) prune type	6	320	3.4
Pokeberry, poke, shoots, raw	0	104	11.8
Potatoes, raw (parings, trimmings)	19	279	7.7

*These numbers indicate approximate percents.

Table 6-1 (continued)

Food and Description (refuse noted in parentheses)	Refuse %	Food Energy cal./lb.	Protein g./lb.
Pumpkins, raw (rind, seeds)	30	83	3.2
Purslane leaves including stems, raw	0	95	7.7
Quinces, raw (parings, core, seeds)	39	158	1.1
Radishes, raw with tops (tops, rootlets, trimmings)	37	49	2.9
Raspberries, raw, black (stems, caps, damaged berries)	3	321	6.6
red (stems, caps, damaged berries)	3	251	5.3
Rhubarb, raw, freshly harvested with full tops (ends, full leaves)	55	33	1.2
Rice, brown, raw	0	1,633	34.0
Rutabagas without tops, raw (parings)	15	177	4.2
Rye, whole grain	0	1,515	54.9
Shallot bulbs, raw (skins)	12*	287	10.0
Sorghum grain, all types	0	1,506	49.9
Soybeans, immature seeds in pods (pods)	47	322	26.2
mature seeds, dry, raw	0	1,828	154.7
Spinach, raw, untrimmed (large stems, roots)	28	85	10.5
Spinach, raw, summer, all varieties (stem ends)	3	84	4.8
winter, all varieties (cavity contents, rind, stem ends)	29	161	4.5
Strawberries, raw (caps, stems)	4	161	3.0

*These numbers indicate approximate percents.

Table 6-1 (continued)

Food and Description (refuse noted in parentheses)	Refuse %	Food Energy cal./lb.	Protein g./lb.
Sunflower seed kernels, dry, in hull (hulls)	46	1,372	58.8
Sweet potatoes, raw (parings, trimmings, damaged spots)	19	419	6.2
Tomatoes, raw, whole	0	100	5.0
Turnips, raw, with tops (tops, rootlets, parings, trimmings)	35	88	2.9
Turnip greens, leaves with stems, raw (discarded leaves)	16	107	11.4
Walnuts, black, in shell (shells)	78	627	20.5
Persian or English in shell (shells)	55	1,329	30.2
Watercress, leaves with stems, raw (stem ends)	8	79	9.2
Watermelon, raw (rind, seeds, cutting loss)	54	54	1.0
Wheat, whole grain, durum	0	1,506	57.6
hard red spring	0	1,497	63.5
hard red winter	0	1,497	55.8
soft red winter	0	1,479	46.3
white	0	1,520	42.6
Wild rice, raw	0	1,601	64.0
Yam, tuber, raw (skin)	14	394	8.2
Yam bean, tuber, raw (parings)	10	225	5.7

Source: Condensed from Watt and Merrill 1963.

Values for food are traditionally stated by scientists in terms of the kilocalorie (kcal.) or large calorie, which is the amount of heat needed to increase the temperature of 1 kilogram of water 1 degree Celsius under normal atmospheric conditions. In food circles this is called a "calorie."

The International Bureau of Weights and Measures recommended that the *joule* be used to describe all forms of energy. The joule is a measure of force over distance currently used to measure electrical, work, and chemical energy. Soon you may be learning that a glass of milk is worth 694½ joules rather than 166 calories.

In that case, remember:

1 kilocalorie = 4.184 kilojoules

or, conversely,

1 kilojoule is about ¼th of a kilocalorie.

Food values can also be described by comparing the amount of protein in the yield. Protein values either are given by weight, computed from percent nitrogen content, or presented in "net protein utilization" units (NPU's), referring to usable protein. For information on NPU values of various foods, see *Diet for a Small Planet* by Francis Moore Lappé (1975).

Table 6-1 gives caloric value and protein content of many of the fruits and vegetables likely to be grown in your garden or on your farm. It is taken from an extensive table labeled "Nutrients in the Edible Portion of 1 Pound of Food as Purchased" in USDA Agriculture Handbook 8, *Composition of Foods* (Watt and Merrill 1963). Since the data were compiled to provide dietary information, some adaptations need to be made for our purposes.

To compute the caloric value of your yield, first find out how many pounds the produce weighs. Next, note the column giving percent refuse. This is the percent of food *as purchased* considered inedible by humans in American culture. Note that "Sweet corn, raw with husk" has 64 percent refuse. This is because corn in season is available without trimmings removed. In computing yield, pick your ears of corn and weigh them before removing the husk, then compute the value of the 36 percent of the edible yield using the table provided. This is done by multiplying 157 calories by number of pounds in yield.

Dry beans are listed as having no refuse. This is because they are usually purchased already shelled. You must shell the beans before weighing to compute yield. The caloric and nutrient calculations are based just on the parts of the plant which are usually eaten. The data give no information as to the value of sweet potato skins, celery leaves, or carrot parings.

The list also includes some wild greens and fruits, so you could do an energetics study comparing wild food collecting with gardening!

Having discussed the producing end of the energetics system, let's talk about the "cultural energy" or what is put into the system. When inputs are primarily those of human labor and small machinery, we are dealing with energy in the magnitude of kilocalories. With heavy use of farm machinery and chemical fertilizers—as on a modern commercial farm—we begin to talk about megacalories (1 megacalorie = 1,000 kilocalories) and perhaps even to disregard the caloric input of human labor.

Table 6-2, "Cultural Energy Conversion Factors," is compiled from a variety of sources; inputs are described in terms of kilocalories. The figures are, of course, just an approximation. For example, fertilizers are produced by many processes, feeds come from both irrigated and non-irrigated areas, water costs vary greatly, and farm equipment has variable efficiency. Each of these alternatives consumes a different quantity of energy.

The energy inputs should be measured over an entire growing season or, better yet, over the entire year to include *all* the work done in preparing the ground, putting in a cover crop, or whatever. Since an accurate energetics balance requires detailed record keeping, do not attempt to quantify your entire gardening effort. Choose an area to study, measure its size and then do all the labor and harvesting of this area separately from the rest of your gardening activities.

(Continued on page 126)

Table 6-2—Cultural Energy Conversion Factors*

Description	Kilocalories of Energy
Draft animal labor (per hr.)	2,400
Human labor (per lb. per 10 min.)	
low level, as in watering lawn	0.162
low-moderate, as in seeding, fertilizing	0.256
moderate, as in raking	0.312
heavy, as in mowing lawn, spading	0.445
Water—will depend on source	
(per gal.)	1.56
(per cu. ft.)	11.70
Chemical fertilizer (per lb.)	
Nitrogen (N)	7,227.27
Phosphorus (P)	1,590.91
Potassium (K)	636.36
Fuels (per gal.)	
gasoline	36,225
diesel fuel	39,416
liquid petroleum gas	24,446
kerosene	39,037
Electricity (per kw. hr.)	2,540
Seed (per lb.)	1,800
Pesticides (per lb.)	
atrazine	20,545
others	15,000
Farm machinery (per ton per mile)	555
Feeds (per ton)	
corn	1,300,000
soybean meal	1,100,000
hay	400,000

*Conversion factors for fuel, machinery, fertilizer, and pesticides were adapted from Johnson et al. 1977.
Note: The ratio of digestible to cultural energy is found by dividing the caloric value of the yield for a given area by the total energy inputs used in its cultivation.

Record of Energy Input

labor		water		machinery			seed	fertilizer
task done	no.10min. units	date	no.cu.ft. or gal.	type	miles	gal. fuel	lbs.	lbs.

Figure 6-1

Keep a notebook or chart handy to record time spent doing each task. The conversion factors for human labor are listed in purposefully small units of 10 minutes. Figure out how many 10-minute periods are spent on a job and multiply that by the kilocalories expended for each pound of body weight. For example, if a 128-pound woman spends 35 minutes turning a compost pile, consider that activity heavy labor similar to mowing a lawn or spading.

Compute:

$$0.445 \text{ kilocalorie} \times 128 \text{ pounds} \times 3\frac{1}{2} \text{ time units} =$$
$$199.36 \text{ kilocalories}$$

To keep track of the energy used in irrigation, you can check the water meter reading before and after watering (water meters measure consumption in cubic feet; be certain no faucets or washing machines are in use at the same time). You can also pour water into gallon containers and use the conversion factor for kilocalories per gallon.

The figures for fertilizers refer to the petrochemical energy used to produce chemical fertilizers. Organic gardeners who apply compost should figure the labor time in collecting and preparing it. If you use organic materials or manures which you must drive a vehicle to collect, figure in kilocalories for the gasoline as well as the cost of the machinery. The latter is calculated by multiplying 555 kilocalories by the number of tons of the vehicle and by the number of miles driven. This calculation is also used for any power equipment, such as a Rototiller.

Prepare a data chart so that you can easily record inputs (see Figure 6-1). Needless to say, if your harvesting is done piecemeal throughout the season, all produce weights should be recorded. Be aware of weather conditions, since differences in temperature and rainfall from year to year affect both energy input and yield.

For more information on energetics and agriculture, see Falk 1976; Heichel 1973; Javits 1977; Johnson et al. 1977; Lappé 1975; Lockeretz 1977; Moorehouse and Juve 1921; Pimentel et al. 1973, 1975, 1976; Rappaport 1971.

7

Slugs, Bugs, and Earthworms

Let's call them "bugs" because that rhymes with "slugs," but really we are talking about all *insects*, not just the one group—the Hemiptera—known as "true bugs."

So there you are, kneeling in your garden, toes pressed into the moist crumbly earth, fingers tamping down the soil around your tomato seedlings . . . the rich tomato-plant smell heavy around you, the sun strong on your back. You luxuriate in the stillness, alone, just you and your plants.

Alone? Not on your life! It is as busy here as in any metropolis. The difference is that your company is quite tiny and, therefore, can easily be overlooked. Overlooked—that is how it usually goes for the millipedes, centipedes, slugs, snails, earthworms, sow bugs, mites, nematodes, spiders, insects, bacteria, and fungi. They live out their lives in and near the soil, generally unnoticed except when, by human standards, something goes awry.

Our knowledge of their goings-on is so incomplete it borders on the superstitious.

Do you care to peer into this cryptic world, to find out more about the lives and livelihoods of the soil invertebrates of your garden? While many of the animals are too small to be studied without a powerful microscope, some are not, and while you will not learn everything about all of them just from studying a few, your powers of observation and reasonable imagination will be enhanced. It will be like traveling and seeing another culture.

In this chapter we will be talking about techniques for working with and experiments you can do with three of the more visible groups of garden invertebrates: slugs, insects, and earthworms. References in the chapter include some sources that will help you to find out more about the other soil microorganisms and animals as well.

SLUGS

Slugs are one kind of garden animal that is large enough to see with the naked eye and to feel with the bare foot. Thus, most of us are highly aware of them, especially if our gardens are in a moist section of the country. Slugs dry out easily and therefore crave damp conditions. That is why one often finds them hiding under the stones and boards of garden walkways by day, waiting for the drying sun to go down before they emerge to devour our vegetables.

If you find slugs to be a problem in your garden, you may want to vary your gardening techniques to see if that would have an effect on the slug population. For example, you could compare the number of slugs found in a non-mulched garden in an open area to the number in a mulched garden or to the number in a garden where boards are used in walkways to avoid soil compaction.

You may wonder how to go about figuring out which slugs are eating up your plants and how many of them are actually doing the work. You can either set out traps for the slugs or you can play sleuth and catch them in the act of devouring your produce.

The best time to observe slugs is on warm, damp, windless evenings when you can go for a walk in your garden, meandering through each experimental plot for a set amount of time (say 15 or 30 minutes), using a flashlight to help you locate the slugs. It is important that the same person make all the observations and that the same flashlight be used on each excursion. These measures are taken to avoid introducing experimental error. The slugs can either simply be observed and counted, or they can be collected for identification (and to rid your garden of them).

The people who first suggested this method in the scientific literature (Barnes and Weil 1944) point out that it is difficult not to have some discrepancy in the amount of searching time spent in each plot because the more slugs there are, the greater the amount of time spent in picking them up and the less time spent in looking for other slugs. The tendency, therefore, is to blunt the more extreme differences in the numbers of slugs counted in the various treatment plots. Another complicating factor is introduced because some species of slugs are harder to see and/or pick up. With these species, more time is devoted to the collection of each individual slug. If you remember these points, however, this remains a valid and straightforward method of evaluating the slug population under different conditions.

Whereas the standardizing feature of the method just described is the amount of time spent in each plot, you could also standardize your effort by using a predetermined number of plants per plot as sampling units. As long as you are consistently diligent in your search of each of the sample plants, the exact amount of time spent per plant is not important. If a plant has few slugs on it or if those that are there are easy to see and collect, you can move on quickly and spend more time at a heavily infested plant.

With these methods of sampling you are not destroying the habitat, so you can return to the same sampling units repeatedly over the season. You might also want to record the yield of your sampling units at the end of the season to correlate slug damage with plant productivity.

The other approach to quantifying the number of of-

Metaldehyde and Bran Slug Trap

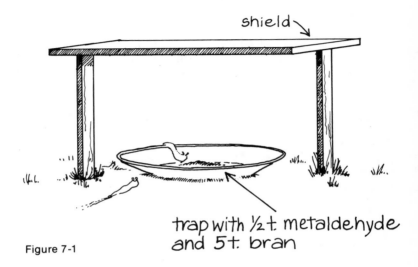

shield

trap with ½ t. metaldehyde
and 5 t. bran

Figure 7-1

fending slugs is to trap them. Your trap can be a board or stone in the center of each sampling area. Each morning overturn the trap to count your catch of resting slugs. Or the trap can be a dish of beer, which some people swear by as an attractant for slugs.

The bait traditionally used by ecologists is a mixture of the poison metaldehyde and bran (½ teaspoon metaldehyde : 5 teaspoons bran per trap). The bran attracts the hungry slugs and the metaldehyde kills them so they do not escape after eating. The traps need to be protected from the rain so the metaldehyde does not wash off or the bran become moldy. You could use a shallow dish for the trap with a wooden or metal shield over it (see Figure 7-1).

Merely setting out any of these traps and counting the results is not enough, however, since you will not know how far the slugs came to get to your trap. You must figure out the area over which the slugs are being attracted under the particular circumstances of your experiment. If you are interested in arriving at complete population density figures rather than just comparing the number of slugs found under different treatment conditions, you must also be able to compute the percentage of slugs within the designated area which respond to your trapping.

To compute the area of attraction, set out four or five traps, all but one of which are ringed by ammonium sulfate at distances varying from 3 to 9 feet from the traps as shown in Figure 7-2. The ammonium sulfate, which serves as a barrier to the slugs, can be purchased from a garden supply store. The idea is that without the barrier the slugs are free to come from as wide an area as they please. You can figure

Slug Trapping Experiment

A ring of ammonium sulfate acts as a barrier to slugs attracted to a baited food-trap. Setting this ring at varying distances from the food-trap, as diagrammed below, helps to establish the radius of the area of attraction.

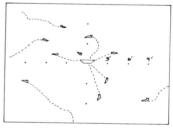

plot 1 : Unrestricted food-baited trap showing area of attraction. Catch : 40 slugs.

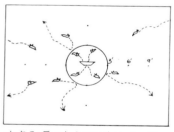

plot 2 : Food-baited trap with ring of ammonium sulfate at 3' from trap. Catch : 25 slugs.

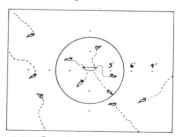

plot 3 : Ring of ammonium sulfate at 5'. Catch: 40 slugs. Conclude, therefore, that this is approximately the distance over which slugs are attracted to unrestricted traps under this set of conditions.

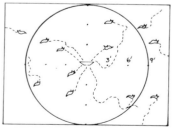

plot 4 : Ring of ammonium sulfate at 9'. Catch : 48 slugs, greater than that at unrestricted trap. Conclude that 9' is probably a greater distance than the slugs will normally travel for food.

Figure 7-2

out how wide an area this is by seeing at which of the other traps your catch is as great as it is at the unrestricted trap. This method was first described in Thomas 1944.

For example, if at your unrestricted trap you capture 40 slugs in one evening and at the trap with a barrier at 3 feet your catch is only 25 slugs with all other conditions being equal, you can conclude that the slugs are being attracted from a greater distance than 3 feet. If the trap with the ammonium sulfate barrier set at 5 feet has a catch equal to that of the unrestricted trap, you can conclude that the slugs are being attracted from a distance of approximately 5 feet.

The ring of ammonium sulfate prevents an influx of migrant slugs. If you set out fresh traps nightly and collect the captured slugs each morning, you should see a decline in the numbers responding to the food-baited traps after several days. If you continue trapping until no more slugs respond, then you can be pretty certain that you have caught virtually all the slugs within the confined area.

Now you can add up each day's catch to find the total number of slugs collected, then compute the percentage that was caught after one day of trapping, two days of trapping, etc.

In this way you can develop an index of the percentage of slugs likely to be captured after a given period of time, thereby cutting down on your work considerably. You will not have to continue trapping until your catch is zero for several days running, but you can assume—as shown in the hypothetical situation tabulated in Figure 7-3—that three days of trapping are sufficient to capture most of the slugs in the area.

These preliminary trials designed to show the area of attraction and the rate of response to the trapping bait must be replicated and otherwise treated as any other experiment in order for their results to be considered valid and for them to be helpful to you in deciding how to proceed with the rest of your experimentation. Replicating your work is especially important since the activity level of slugs—and, therefore, their response to food baits—is greatly affected by differing weather conditions.

Most slugs are surface feeders, eating the above-ground

Example of Data Sheet from Slug Trapping Experiment

treatment	replication	day	1	2	3	4	5	6	7	total
					number of slugs trapped					
backyard garden with many hiding places	1		43	37	17	8	3	0	0	108
	2		39	32	19	6	1	2	0	99
	3		41	30	14	2	0	1	0	88
	total		123	99	50	16	4	3	0	295
	mean		41	33	17	5	1	1	0	98
	range		4	7	5	6	2	2	0	20
garden in open field	1									
	2									

Using the mean values, divide 41 by 98 to find the percentage of slugs captured after 1 day trapping: $\frac{41}{98}$ (100) = percentage slugs trapped in one day
$$= 42\%$$
Add the catch of the first 3 days (41 + 33 + 17) and divide by 98 to find the percentage caught: $\frac{41 + 33 + 17}{98}$ (100) =
$$\frac{91}{98} = 93\%$$
Thus, as you can see, 3 days of trapping is sufficient to collect most of the slugs in this hypothetical situation.

Figure 7-3

portion of plants, but some slugs live in the soil and feed on roots. To trap these subsurface feeders as they are working, you can take a soil sample and go through it by hand. Your sample should be 1 foot deep since the subterranean slugs are virtually all found within the top 12 inches of soil.

To find out which species of slug is devastating your crop, you can use the very clearly illustrated field guide *How to Know the Eastern Land Snails* by John B. Burch (1962). Identification is for the most part based on characteristics which can be seen with the naked eye or with the help of a 10x hand lens.

For further reading about slugs, see Barnes and Weil 1942, 1945, and Newell 1971.

WORKING WITH INSECTS

Pest management—how to control those problem insects—is an intriguing subject for the curious investigator. Understanding the complexities of biological control[1] is like unraveling a mystery story with little clues, diversions, and setbacks all along the way. There is no reason that the conscientious backyard researcher cannot play a part in revealing some of the mystery. Much of the fundamental work involves careful observation of an insect without requiring fancy equipment.

What is necessary is a familiarity with the techniques of entomology (the study of insects) so that you can rear immature insects to adulthood; trap, capture, and mark insects for observation; kill them for collection purposes; and label and store your collection properly for future reference. We will be talking about these techniques in this section.

Since there are nearly one million species of insects found in North America alone, the research methods suggested here will not, of course, be equally applicable for all. Do not be surprised to begin working and find yourself developing a technique that was not mentioned in this section. This is how the enormous body of entomological literature now existing has evolved. You might find it worth your while, in fact, to tap the fruits of some of this earlier research wQrk. Follow the step-by-step approach to using a research library which is presented in Chapter 2. Since it is often necessary to send insect specimens to professional entomologists to verify the identifications you have made, see especially Step 9, "Personal Contacts," which talks about getting in touch with experts in particular fields.

Books and articles about insects cited here and found in the bibliography should also be of help to you. They fall into three sometimes overlapping categories.

1. Those which deal with technique. These can be articles in research journals written by the person(s) who developed the technology or syntheses of methods, often found in book form. You may want to see Borror et al. 1976; Galtsoff et al. 1937; Levi 1966;

Peterson 1964; Reed and Webb 1975; Schwartz 1975, 1977; Yearbook of Agriculture, *Insects* 1952.

2. Guides for the gardener or farmer which identify the better-known problem insects by species. You look in the index under the name of the vegetable, fruit, or flower being bothered and are referred to a list and description of the insect(s) thay may be at the root of the problem. While you must be careful that your specimen is, in fact, the insect being discussed, these reference sources are invaluable in rapidly identifying specific pests, a process that would otherwise be very time-consuming for you.

The biological information is often rather vague, however, so as to cover the full range of possibilities if the insect hails from over a wide geographical area. It might say, for example, that a species has from one to three generations per year depending on the length of the frost-free period. This does not tell you much about when you can expect it to be found in the larval stage gobbling up leafy greens in your garden. Your backyard observations of the insect's life cycle may very likely be the first ones made in your geographical area. You might try rearing some of the insects in captivity as a sure way to be able to collect all of the life stages and also as an aid in making your observations.

3. General entomological field guides and texts which use keys and/or illustrations to help you identify insects to the family level.[2] Insects within one family, while having a great deal in common, can also be quite diverse, so this is actually just the first step in figuring out the biological characteristics of the insect you are dealing with. (Only when you are talking about a particular species of insect can you make valid statements about its life cycle and habits.) These general texts can refer you to more specific reference sources with which insects can be keyed to generic and species levels. These, however, are often quite difficult to work with and would probably not

make much sense to anyone other than a professional entomologist.

Some references which identify specific insect pests or which are good general keys to insects and other invertebrates are: Baker 1972; Borror et al. 1976; Borror and White 1970; Chiang 1977; Davidson and Peairs 1966; Eddy and Hodson 1961; Kaston 1948; Kaston and Kaston 1978; Metcalf, Flint, and Metcalf 1962; Pennak 1953; Peterson 1948, 1951; Reed and Webb 1975; Schwartz 1975, 1977; Usinger 1956; Westcott 1973; and Yearbook of Agriculture, *Insects* 1952.

Rearing Insects

There are several reasons for attempting to rear insects and other arthropods. Most keys to identification are based on the adult stage, partly because larvae and other immature forms have fewer identifying features, and partly because they have not been as well studied as the adults. Thus, even if you know that it is a skinny little yellowish maggot tunneling through your carrots, and even if the guides to garden pests suggest that an animal of this description and habits is the carrot rust fly *(Psila rosae)*, it is only by rearing the maggot and identifying the rather harmless and short-lived adult that you can know for sure.

By keeping your insect colony alive through all life stages, you will end up with a series of specimens of the egg, larvae, pupae, and adult (as long as you remember to collect and preserve samples from each of these stages). With careful observation and record keeping, the whole life story of the insect can be told: how long the larval stage lasts, how many times the larvae molt and shed their skin, physical or behavioral differences between the various larval instars[3] the amount of food each of these insects can eat, where and for how long pupation occurs, and on and on. It may very well take generations in the life of your insect culture before you are able to figure out the answers to these and any other questions you are interested in.

There are two points to keep in mind. First, the behavioral patterns, length of each developmental stage, and sometimes even the physical appearance of the same insect species can vary from one generation to the next depending on the time of year. The rosy apple aphid (*Dysaphis plantaginea*) is an extreme example. It spends the winter on apple twigs in the egg stage. Come early spring the eggs hatch out to wingless females which reproduce parthenogenetically (reproduction from unfertilized eggs), creating another generation of wingless females. These produce a generation of winged females which migrate to narrow-leaved plantain. Once settled, several more generations of fatherless females without wings are created over the summer months. As autumn approaches, winged aphids of both sexes are produced to make the trip back to the apple tree where they mate and the females lay eggs which over-winter. It obviously took a lot of careful watching to figure this one out!

The second point to be aware of is that insects may react differently in captivity than they do normally. Thus you should make every effort to have the conditions in the rearing cages just like home for them. You should compare the activities of the captive insects with what is going on in the field.

Cold temperatures and a decreasing food supply are often the signals that tell an insect it is time to get ready for winter. If you provide food for your insect culture and keep it indoors, you can perhaps keep it alive over the winter, which is a valuable technique—if that is your intention. Obviously you cannot draw any conclusions about the insect's life cycle from this arrangement, however.

Another reason for rearing insects is to see if a garden pest has any parasitoid enemies. Parasitoids, which are usually smaller insects developing within a larger insect by living off its body contents, are an important factor in biological control (see Figure 7-4).

Perhaps you have heard the phenomenal statistics about how we would be wallowing knee-deep in insects if one pair of highly fecund flies reproduced at their normal rate and their offspring did the same, all with a 100 percent survival rate. Since this is not the case, it is clear that most

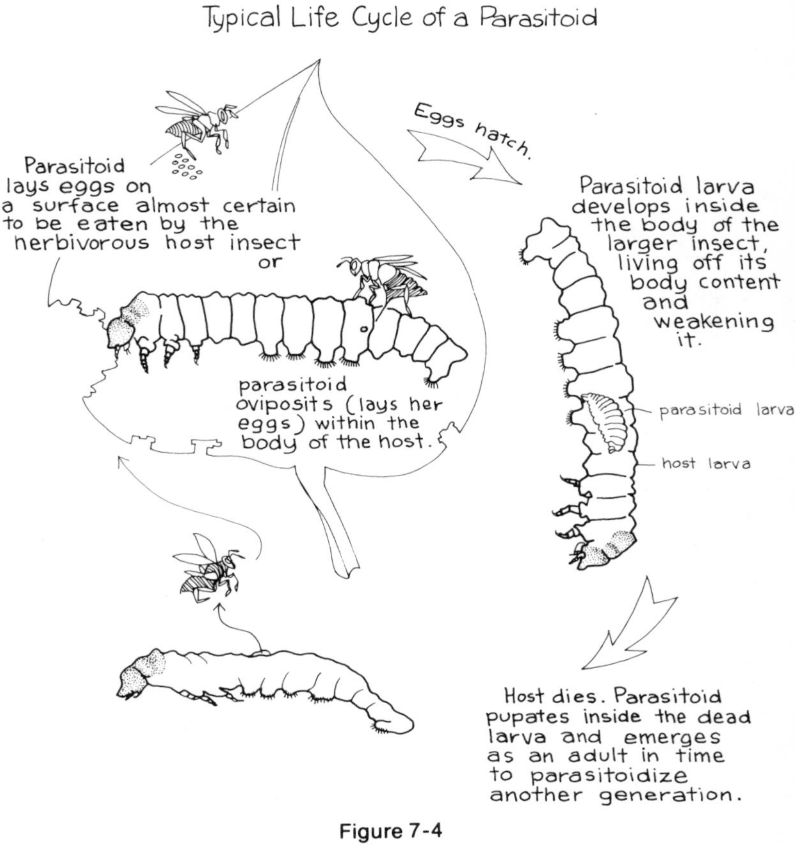

Typical Life Cycle of a Parasitoid

Parasitoid lays eggs on a surface almost certain to be eaten by the herbivorous host insect

or

Eggs hatch.

Parasitoid larva develops inside the body of the larger insect, living off its body content and weakening it.

parasitoid oviposits (lays her eggs) within the body of the host.

parasitoid larva

host larva

Host dies. Parasitoid pupates inside the dead larva and emerges as an adult in time to parasitoidize another generation.

Figure 7-4

insect eggs never survive to adulthood. They die from a variety of causes: weather conditions; predation by birds, small mammals, spiders, or other insects; viral and bacterial diseases which tend to strike when the population density of an insect species gets too high; starvation; or parasitoids. These factors work in concert to keep the population of each species in balance. That is why problem insects are usually those imported from afar without their normal entourage of natural enemies.

If you find pupal cases with small holes in them, these small holes may very likely have been made by emerging parasitoids. With this as a clue, you can collect larvae of the next generation and keep them in captivity. If any insect emerges other than the adult you are expecting and if your culture is pure, you can pretty certainly conclude that the unexpected insects are parasitoids. Other parasitoids attack and develop within the larvae of their hosts, preventing them from ever reaching the pupal stage.

If you find that an insect pest does have parasitoid enemies, you could embark on the ambitious project of rearing parasitoids in large numbers for a release-and-control program. Before doing this, I would suggest you do some reading on the theory of biological control as well as the success and failure stories of previous efforts.

Rearing Chambers

There are probably as many varieties of rearing chambers as there are people with imaginations involved with this sort of thing. Four types are described here.

The most effective rearing chambers are those which least alter natural conditions. With some plants it is possible to set up an enclosure around all or part of the plant, thereby preventing the insects from going elsewhere without disturbing the normal development of either plant or insect. Make a wooden or wire framework and cover it with netting of an appropriate weave to contain the insects in which you are interested (see Figure 7-5). If the insect whose life cycle you are charting is known or thought to leave the plant and pupate in soil or leaf litter, you may want to put a layer of leaves or soil in the bottom of the cage.

Since you do not want to be providing a home for all the soil insects as well (including possibly predators and disease carriers), you can sterilize the soil by heating it to 220°F. in your oven for about an hour. Any time you want to limit your rearing efforts to just those creatures which you introduce into the system, the growing medium should be sterilized. But be aware that by doing this you are altering the dynamics of the system. It would perhaps be interesting to sterilize the contents of one of your rearing cages but not another and compare the results.

With some plants and insects it may not be possible (or desirable) to use a rearing chamber in the field. In these

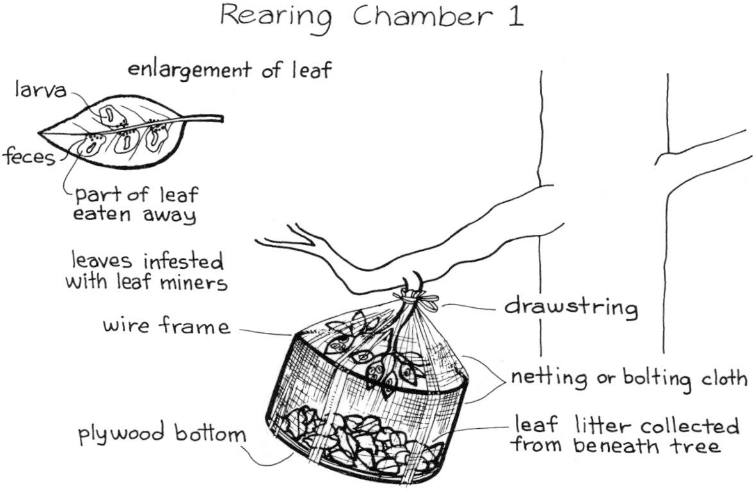

Rearing Chamber 1

Figure 7-5

cases try to simulate natural conditions within a gallon jar or a terrarium. If needed, have a layer of sterilized soil or leaves on the bottom. Put a sample of the host plant in a small jar of water. A piece of cardboard over the jar with a hole for the stem of the plant will prevent insects from falling in the water and drowning (see Figure 7-6). Predaceous insects and spiders can also be reared in this way by providing them with other insects to eat and some sticks and debris for them to climb about on.

For burrowing insects, you can take the habitat—whether it be a root vegetable, the soil, or some compost—put it into a glass container with netting on top, and keep it at its accustomed level of moisture, light, and temperature. To keep the insects in the dark, as they would be underground, wrap the chamber in a cylinder of heavy paper which can be easily slipped off for observation (see Figure 7-7). Since adult insects are usually attracted to the light (it guides them out of the soil as they emerge into adulthood, into the air where they can fly and mate and begin a new cycle of life), you may want to have part of the chamber exposed to light, as shown in Figure 7-7.

Some small, nonflying insects can be observed right on

Rearing Chamber 2

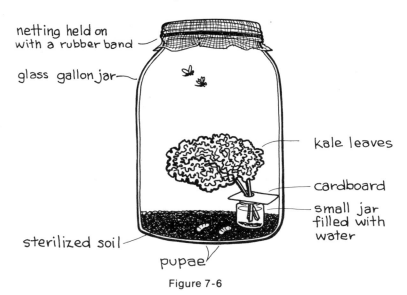

netting held on
with a rubber band

glass gallon jar

kale leaves

cardboard

small jar
filled with
water

sterilized soil

pupae

Figure 7-6

Rearing Chambers 3a. and 3b.

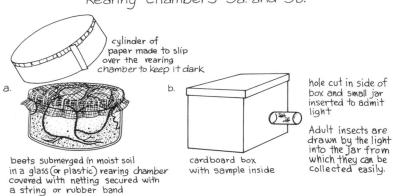

cylinder of
paper made to slip
over the rearing
chamber to keep it dark

a.

b.

hole cut in side of
box and small jar
inserted to admit
light

Adult insects are
drawn by the light
into the jar from
which they can be
collected easily.

beets submerged in moist soil
in a glass (or plastic) rearing chamber
covered with netting secured with
a string or rubber band

cardboard box
with sample inside

Figure 7-7

the host plant by ringing their eating locale with "Tanglefoot," a sticky substance used for trapping insects. The ring
prevents migrations, so you know that you are following the
development of the same group of insects (see Figure 7-8).

Rearing Chamber 4
(Redrawn from Borror, DeLong, and Triplehorn 1976)

ring of Tanglefoot

hole in leaf

insect larvae

Figure 7-8

Food Preference Chambers

Figuring out food preferences is still another incentive to get involved with rearing insects in captivity. Certain plants, for some reason or other (chemical compounds, color, texture, etc.), are found desirable by insects, while others seem to be resistant to their attack. By providing a captured insect with a variety of foods, you may be able to determine which ones are actively sought after by healthy insects, which are merely tolerated by the hungry, which will barely sustain the insect while perhaps causing it to lose its vigor or ability to reproduce, and which foods will not be tolerated even at the cost of starvation.

From this point you may be able to determine which factors of resistance are at play and then devise a method to discourage insect attack. (An excellent source on this subject is Painter 1951.)

Figures 7-9 and 7-10 illustrate two types of food preference chambers—one which brings food of various types to caged insects and the other which brings insects to caged plants. For the former, take samples of leaves from different plants (they can be of different species, different varieties of the same species, the same variety grown under different conditions, or simply samples from the same plot, depending on what you are trying to test) and put them in a container housing the insects. Fresh leaves can be supplied frequently or you can try to maintain the samples in a fresh state by keeping the stems in water. By knowing how many

Food Preference Chamber

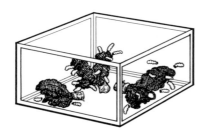

Samples of different plants in a terrarium are kept moist by wrapping with wet paper towel and foil.

See which plant is the preferred food by measuring the amount of each sample consumed and by seeing where the insects are congregated.

Figure 7-9

insects are in the chamber and how much of a sample was consumed, you can compute feeding rates as well as food preferences.

To do this, weigh or measure (using the method of counting squares described in Chapter 3, Box 3-7) the amount of food given to the insects. Subtract the amount remaining after a given period of time to find the amount consumed. Divide this by the number of insects which were eating that sample to find the feeding rate per insect. By comparing feeding rates during different periods of the day, you can determine if the insect is a diurnal or nocturnal feeder. Of course, before you draw any conclusions, your experiment must be replicated several times.

Years ago a food preference experiment supplying gypsy moth larvae with leaves from different species of trees was conducted in this way. The results of that test have been used ever since to predict the amount of damage that the gypsy moth will likely cause in forests of differing species composition.

The second type of chamber (see Figure 7-10) encloses samples of different plants in separate compartments with a passageway in between. The samples can be parts of plants, but are preferably whole plants, with the experiment conducted right in the field or in a greenhouse. A field experiment can be continued uninterrupted over a longer period of time than an experiment where you must periodically

Food Preference Experiment

netting on wire framework

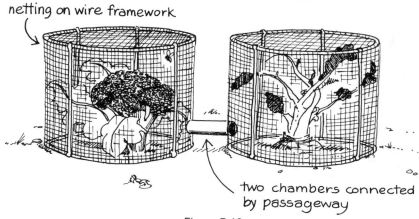

two chambers connected
by passageway

Figure 7-10

replace old foodstuffs with fresh. The number of herbivorous (plant-eating) insects in each chamber is counted at intervals to see which plant is the preferred food. This type of food preference chamber is described in Rateaver et al. 1975.

Collecting Insects

To find out which insects are which, first you will have to catch them. Insect-collecting equipment is standard fare at several of the supply houses listed in Appendix I, but if you wish to do so, much of it can be homemade. For general collecting you need a collecting net, various jars, and, perhaps, forceps, a small brush, and a magnifying lens.

A collection net can be purchased from a supply house or can be homemade. I made an unorthodox but satisfactory net by unstringing a badminton racket and sewing on netting from an old mesh curtain through the preexisting holes in the racket rim (see Figure 7-11). However, this net is not quite big enough nor is the handle quite long enough for all purposes.

For a standard-size net, use 2½ to 3 feet of an old broomstick for the handle and 3¼ feet of 6- to 8-gauge wire

Badminton Racket Net

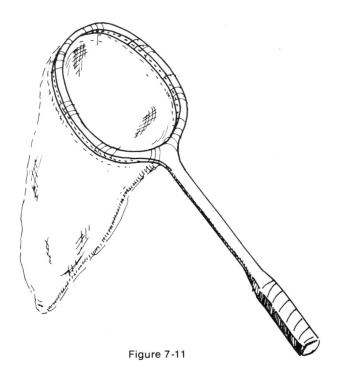

Figure 7-11

to make a rim 1 foot in diameter. To attach the rim to the frame, bend it as shown in Figure 7-12, drill the holes in the broom handle as shown, and secure it with a metal band or heavy tape. The bag itself should be about twice as long as its diameter, approximately 2 feet long.

Muslin is often used for the part closest to the rim to give the bag strength. The rest of the bag is a fine netting like bolting cloth or the mosquito netting sold in sporting goods stores for tent flaps. The holes should be small enough to contain even very small flies but large enough so that you can see what is inside.

The net can be swung randomly, with the catch from a set number of sweeps as your sample if you are doing a population survey, or you can place the net over a plant and

Standard-Size Collecting Net

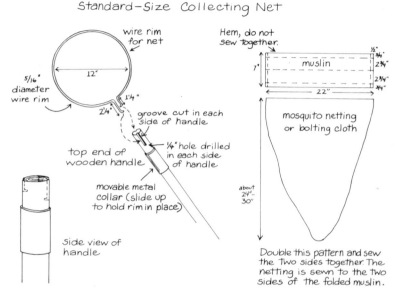

Figure 7-12

collect samples of all the trapped insects (see Figure 7-13). To remove your catch from the net, put a collecting jar up into the net and tap the insects into it, or use forceps to transfer the insects.

Forceps are available from many of the biological supply houses; they are standard equipment in dissecting kits. Fine forceps, which are invaluable when dealing with minute insects, can also be purchased from surgical or jewelers' supply houses. Alvah Peterson, whose book *Entomological Techniques: How to Work with Insects* (1964) is a gem, even suggests you can make your own fine forceps by cutting them out of a tin can like a coffee can. Cut a strip 6 to 8 inches long by ⅜ inch wide, bend it in half and cut the ends to points.

Small, dampened watercolor brushes are very helpful for picking up small insects and other small creatures since they adhere to the bristles. One of the most enjoyable pieces of equipment to have on a collecting expedition is a 10x magnifier loupe, available from most of the supply houses.

Transferring Insects from the Collecting Net to a Killing Jar

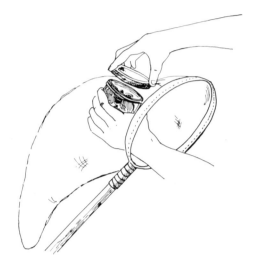

Slide one hand, holding the jar, into the bag, trapping the insect.

The other hand, holding the jar cover, is on the outside of the bag. Put the cover over the jar until the insect is stunned, then slide the jar out of the bag and screw on the jar top.

Figure 7-13

Once you have used one of these magnifiers, you will never want to go for a walk without this extra-powerful eye.

Methods of Killing Insects

Once you have collected the insects, you can either look at them and let them go; put them in rearing chambers; or kill them so that they can be identified and saved for future reference.

Adult insects can be killed by putting them in a freezer, or by immersing them in small containers in boiling water which exposes them to dry heat for 5 to 20 seconds.

Another method is to expose them to toxic fumes. Several chemicals can be used to supply the fumes. Entomologists usually use cyanide as the poison, making up a jar as shown in Figure 7-14. They use cyanide purchased from a biological supply house. Although most supply houses will not sell this or other chemicals to individuals, you can

Cyanide Insect Killing Jar

absorbent paper strips

¼"–½" dried plaster of paris (pour in ½"–1" wet)

¼" layer powdered cyanide (can be mixed with sawdust)

Wrap masking tape around jar and write "POISON."

To test potency of jar, wave fumes toward your nose; do not smell jar directly.

Figure 7-14

buy the jars already made up. Either calcium cyanide, sodium cyanide, or potassium cyanide can be used; the toxin in each is hydrogen cyanide, a gas formed in the presence of moisture.

All of the cyanide killing jars have a finite life span, which can be prolonged by keeping them tightly capped and dry inside. Crumpled paper towel strips help keep the jar dry by absorbing moisture (the strips should be changed frequently) and create a labyrinth, making it difficult for the captured insects to escape. To see if your jar is still potent after a period of disuse, open it and wave the air above it toward you. If it still smells, it is still potent. Do not stick your nose in the jar to smell it directly.

Insects should be removed from the cyanide jars soon after they are killed; otherwise, they will get brittle. To keep the insects pliable, store them in a "relaxing jar" made from a large peanut butter jar with several inches of moist sand on the bottom (see Figure 7-15). Above the sand put a platform of some sort—you could use the plastic top to a cottage cheese container. Make pinholes all over the platform so moisture can circulate. A mothball taped to the side of the jar will retard spoilage.

Ethyl acetate (acetic ether) jars, which also can be purchased from biological supply houses, are safer to use than the cyanide jars, but slower working and much shorter-lived. They can be recharged easily, however, unlike the cyanide jars.

To make your own jar (see Figure 7-16) to use with either chemical, take a wide-mouth bottle of about pint size. Wrap it with masking tape so it will not shatter if broken, and write POISON on the tape and on the top of the jar. For an ethyl acetate jar pour in about ½-inch of plaster of paris, let it set, and then dry in the oven at low temperature. When dry, add enough ethyl acetate to saturate the plaster (expect to recharge it after several days' use). To recharge, dry out

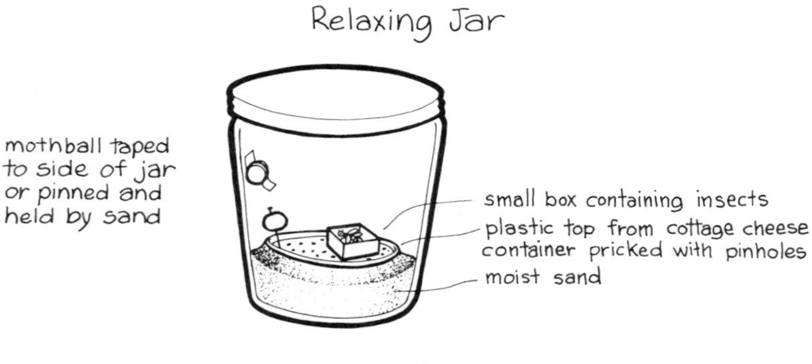

Relaxing Jar

mothball taped to side of jar or pinned and held by sand

small box containing insects
plastic top from cottage cheese container pricked with pinholes
moist sand

Figure 7-15

Ethyl Acetate Jar

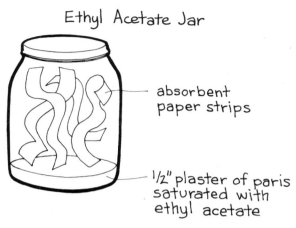

absorbent
paper strips

½" plaster of paris
saturated with
ethyl acetate

Figure 7-16

the jar in the oven and saturate the plaster again with ethyl acetate. Insects can be kept in these jars almost indefinitely since this chemical keeps them pliable without allowing them to spoil.

Alvah Peterson suggests using cigarette lighter fluid to provide the toxic fumes. This is actually V.M. and P. naptha, a high grade of benzene used for thinning paint and for dry cleaning.

Butterflies and moths should be kept separate from other insects, as they tend to beat their wings madly in captivity, showering everything with their wing scales. The paper towel strips cushion the damage, but you should also squeeze their bodies to immobilize them before they go into the killing jar. Larger insects, especially beetles which take a long time before they succumb, should be kept separate from small, delicate insects.

Immature insects and small or soft-bodied adults can be put directly into a liquid killing solution. You can use 70 to 90 percent ethyl alcohol or 40 to 70 percent isopropyl alcohol in water (available in a drugstore), although both have a tendency to discolor the larvae. Immature insects can be killed by placing them in very hot water (near the boiling point) and keeping them there until the water cools. Then transfer them to a 25 percent ethyl alcohol solution for an hour, then to a 50 percent solution for an hour, and then to a 70 percent solution for permanent storage.

If you have the chemicals available, a solution recommended for killing immatures called KAAD can be made as follows:

1 part kerosene (less for soft-bodied larvae)

7 to 10 parts 95 percent ethyl alcohol

2 parts glacial acetic acid

1 part dioxane.

After half an hour to four hours, the insects killed in this way are ready to be transferred to an alcohol storage solution.

Extracting Insects

Another approach to collecting insects, especially small ones, is to take a sample of their habitat (soil, compost, litter, vegetables, rotting logs, fungi, etc.) and extract the insects from it. You can try to maintain the habitat in near-normal conditions and rear the insects to adulthood, capturing them as they emerge (use a rearing chamber like those shown earlier in this chapter). Or you can use a "modified Berlese or Tullgren extraction funnel." With the extraction funnel the sample is dried slowly, driving the insects out in search of moisture and eventually into a collecting jar placed beneath the funnel.

You can make a funnel of any size by wrapping some heavy paper or metal into a cone shape or you can use a wide-mouth plastic funnel or a plastic beaker with the bottom cut out (see Figure 7-17). Inside the funnel put two circles of wire mesh, first a heavy ¼- to ½-inch mesh to support your sample and above this a fine hardware cloth to screen out dirt particles. The sample is placed above the screening.

To dry the sample evenly, it may be helpful to break up the larger clods. While you are doing this, you can pick out the larger invertebrate animals—such as earthworms, snails, large insects, sow bugs—or any forms that are in a passive stage like eggs, pupae, or hibernating adults. For the first 24 hours let the sample air dry. After that you can place a

Extraction Funnels

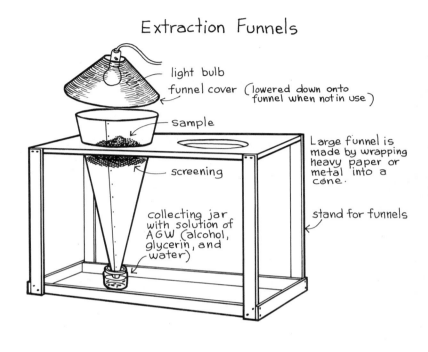

light bulb

funnel cover (lowered down onto funnel when not in use)

sample

Large funnel is made by wrapping heavy paper or metal into a cone.

screening

collecting jar with solution of AGW (alcohol, glycerin, and water)

stand for funnels

Smaller plastic funnels are supported by the collecting jar itself or by a wire stand or by a stand similar to the one shown above.

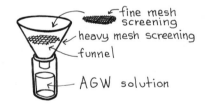

fine mesh screening

heavy mesh screening

funnel

AGW solution

Figure 7-17

low-wattage (7½ watt) bulb above the sample to help dry it from the top down. Small samples can be dried without the light, but all samples should have some sort of netting over the top of the funnel so that emerging adults do not fly away. Keep the apparatus in place for about a week or until the sample is thoroughly dry.

If the numbers and types of insects collected in one sample are to be compared with those collected in other samples, then the size of all the samples must be equal and all must be treated alike. If larger creatures are handpicked from one of the samples, then they should be handpicked from all; if a light bulb is used to dry one of the samples, the same wattage light bulb should be used for all the samples; if one sample is dried for seven days, the others should be also.

The reason this uniformity is important is that no one extraction system effectively removes all the animals. Which creatures are extracted depends very much on how the sample is handled. Your data would be biased if some samples were treated differently than others.

Of course you can group the samples, using a different extraction method for each group. Then only the samples within a particular group would be compared with one another. In total this would give you more information than you would get from using the same extraction method on all the samples.

To collect the animals, tape a jar to the mouth of the funnel as shown in Figure 7-17. In the jar have a solution of 70 percent alcohol, 30 percent water, plus a very small amount of glycerin which prevents the animals from drying out even if all the alcohol should evaporate.

This extraction method is used to collect mites and spiders as well as insects. Mites are very small animals which are related to spiders and are very important in the decomposition cycle. One needs a powerful microscope to be able to see them clearly, however, so they are not very good guinea pigs for the backyard researcher.

Trapping Insects

Trapping insects on a surface coated with "Tanglefoot" is another approach to collecting insects. Tanglefoot is a nonreactive sticky substance the consistency of petroleum jelly. It can be removed with any hand cleaner and does not need to be heated before using, unlike some of the other sticky gums used to trap insects. It is sold at garden supply stores, where homeowners buy it to catch larval defoliators crawling up and down the trunks of their ornamental trees.

The tree itself attracts the insects: the Tanglefoot just traps them—by itself it has no attractant properties. To use it in an agricultural experiment or as a tool in pest control, you must first figure out how to attract the insects in large numbers.

Starting with the basics, you must have some idea of the life cycle of the insect in question. Where does it spend the different stages of its life? Doing what—eating leaves, looking for food, looking for a mate, looking for a place to lay its eggs, looking for a host to parasitoidize, buzzing after flowers? What colors, shapes, or odors guide the insect to the place where it can meet its needs? Something, after all, must be a signal to the adult apple maggot (*Rhagoletis pomonella*, family Tephritidae) to let it know that it is approaching an apple tree.

For a week and a half after the adult apple maggot emerges from its pupal case in the soil beneath an apple tree, it flies about drinking the liquid from foliage. Then it is drawn to apples, where it mates and lays its eggs. So it makes sense that the flies would first be attracted to a trap that looks or smells like foliage and later to one that looks or smells like apples. Using these clues a group of researchers (Kring 1970) developed several trap designs which they tested against one another to see which were the most effective. A sticky gum was painted over the traps to capture the insects.

Different-size panels of yellow-painted exterior plywood set to face in different directions were used separately and in combination with 3-inch red spheres, hemispheres, disks, and spots (see Figure 7-18). The trap with the red sphere mounted on yellow plywood and facing to the south attracted the greatest number of flies. The traps were placed within the canopy of the apple trees, about 6 feet off the ground, either on stands or hung from tree branches with wire.

The trapping program was not completely successful in that not all of the apple maggot flies in the area were captured. The researchers speculated as to why this may have been: as the insects grew older and more sexually mature, their responsiveness to visual stimuli may have decreased;

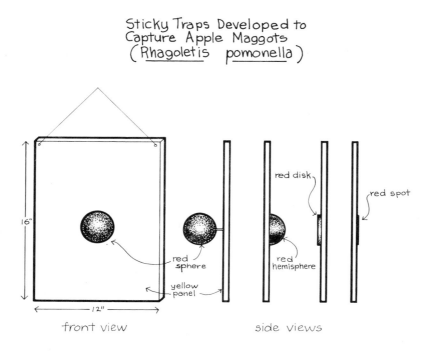

Sticky Traps Developed to
Capture Apple Maggots
(<u>Rhagoletis</u>   <u>pomonella</u>)

Figure 7-18

flies that got to the real apples first could not muster the
enthusiasm necessary to be drawn to a wooden replica (once
their eggs were laid, their interest in apples may have
waned); and some individuals just did not respond to these
stimuli.

Perhaps the effectiveness of the stimuli could be increased with further refinements on the design of the traps.
For example, during midsummer when the eggs are laid,
most apples are still at least partially green. Green or green
and red wooden spheres might be more attractive to the
flies than the dark red spheres.

With any system of pest control, timing is very important. In the case of the apple maggot, trapping is most effective if done before the flies have mated and laid the eggs to
start a new generation. Thus the yellow panels to which the

flies are attracted during the first week and a half of their adult life are vital to the success of the control program even though, in terms of numbers alone, they do not attract as many flies as the red spheres.

The real effect of any pest control program is measured by evaluating its influence on the population dynamics of the insect. Does partial elimination of one generation decrease the size of the following generations, or does it merely lessen the competitive pressures so that a greater proportion of the young of the new generation survives?

To work out the intricacies of a pest management program is to solve a fascinating and complex puzzle! Rather than being overwhelmed by it all, the backyard researcher can begin to work on one question at a time, beginning perhaps with figuring out which colors are most attractive to specific insects. The trap design shown in Figure 7-19 has proven effective in several experiments testing color preference. The experimental variables are the different colors painted on the cans.

You could, in addition, vary the location of the traps so that some of them are visible to the insect only at close range (as would be the case with traps in among tall plants or in an orchard or woodlot) and others are visible from greater distances (such as those in an open field). In this way you could determine if a color is equally attractive at all distances or if, perhaps, odor, shape, or motion are more of an attractive stimulus at some distances.

Working on color preference experiments may arouse your interest in the color perception ability of insects. Read the fascinating books of Nobel laureate Karl von Frisch who pioneered in the experimental work on honeybee behavior. He conducted tests of color perception which are simple enough to be replicated by any of us (von Frisch 1971; see also Miller et al. 1968).

The traps used to test for the color preference of an insect are not likely to be effective pest control devices by themselves. That is because the trap, no matter how attractive its color, is still in competition with the "real thing"—whatever it was that the insect was looking for when drawn to the trap. To be an effective control device,

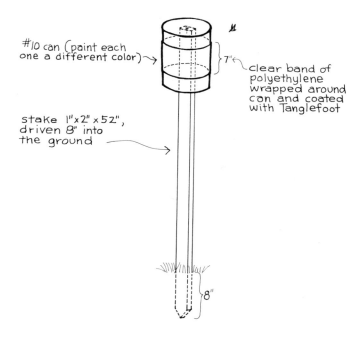

Sticky Trap Design for
Color Preference Tests
(Adapted from Alverson, All, and Matthews 1977)

#10 can (paint each
one a different color)

clear band of
polyethylene
wrapped around
can and coated
with Tanglefoot

7"

stake 1"x2"x52",
driven 8" into
the ground

8"

Figure 7-19

the trap will have to be made *more* attractive than the normal food source, mating place, or mate. To have this much appeal, the trap will probably need to offer the combined attractant qualities of color, shape, and chemicals.

For example, the inverted can trap shown in Figure 7-20 was adapted for an experiment designed to capture all the blackflies in a particular area. The cans were painted a dark shiny blue and were used in conjunction with carbon dioxide gas as the attractants. Since vertebrate animals give off carbon dioxide as they breathe, blackflies and other biting flies are attracted to the gas because it often shows them where to find their potential food source. The source of the

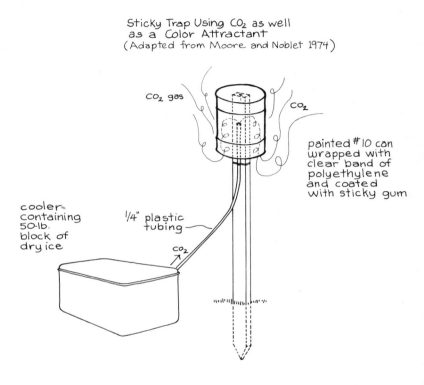

Sticky Trap Using CO₂ as well
as a Color Attractant
(Adapted from Moore and Noblet 1974)

Figure 7-20

carbon dioxide used for this experiment was a 50-pound block of dry ice kept in a Styrofoam cooler beneath the sticky trap. A ¼-inch plastic tube led from the Styrofoam container to the inside of the inverted can, from which point the gas diffused up and around the can.

On a very sophisticated level, pheromones—which are chemicals given off by insects and probably by most other animals as signals to members of their own species—are being isolated and synthesized in laboratories to be used as bait for collection traps. Pheromone-baited traps coated with Tanglefoot have been developed to trap the smaller European elm bark beetle (*Scolytus multistriatus*, family

159

Scolytidae), carrier of the Dutch elm disease, which has caused the loss of many of the once-common American elms.

Preserving Insects

Adult insects can be preserved on special thin, nonrusting insect pins. Although there is a precise place to stick the pin through each type of insect, the basic idea is to put the pin vertically through the right side of the thorax (the segments bearing the legs), obscuring as little of the body of the insect as possible (see Figure 7-21). The pin goes through the right side rather than through the middle because there is a left side very much like the right side, but there is only one middle and you would not want to ruin it with a pinhole.

Below the insect on the pin go two identification labels. When preparing insects for a standard "museum" reference collection, the labels each are put at a uniform height by using a "pinning block." This is a small rectangle of wood with three holes drilled in it at depths of 1 inch, ¾ inch, and ½ inch. The pin with just the insect on it is put into the 1-inch hole, which pushes the insect up to the correct height—1 inch from the bottom of the pin. When the first

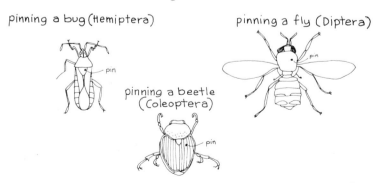

Pinning Insects

pinning a bug (Hemiptera)

pinning a fly (Diptera)

pin

pinning a beetle
(Coleoptera)

pin

pin

Figure 7-21

Pinning Block Used for Museum Reference Collection

pinning block

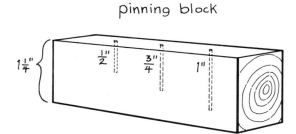

fly and 2 labels on an insect pin

Figure 7-22

label is put on, the pin goes into the second hole, pushing the label up to ¾ inch from the bottom of the pin. The pin with the insect and both labels is, lastly, put into the ½-inch hole so that the lower label is pushed up to that height (see Figure 7-22).

The standard labels are very small (¼ inch by ¾ inch) and should be cut from heavy paper with a high rag content. To fit all the necessary information on the labels, you need to use a very fine point pen, such as a Staedtler Mars 700 drafting pen, size 000 or 0000. A fine-point quill pen with India ink can also be used. Your name, as collector, and the date and location (city or town, county, and state) where the insect was found go on the first label. On the second label, describe the habitat in which the insect was found, such as "reared from potato" or "in compost 3 feet below surface."

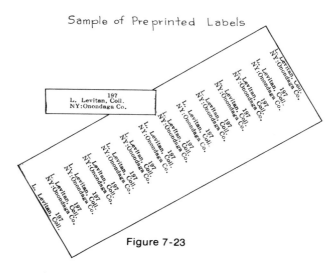

Sample of Preprinted Labels

197
L. Levitan, Coll.
NY:Onondaga Co.

Figure 7-23

Be as specific as possible on both labels and do not abbreviate, since ambiguous abbreviations can cause confusion later. The value of your collection is lost without this ecological information, so you should be sure to have it on record even if your labels do not meet museum specifications. You can purchase partially preprinted labels, as shown in Figure 7-23, from Insect Museum Supply, listed with the suppliers in Appendix I. If you are going to be doing a lot of collecting in one area, preprinted labels save a lot of time.

Very small insects can also be pinned, using some modifications of the pinning methods as shown in Figure 7-24. You can put the pin through a small triangle of stiff paper (called a "point") and then glue the insect to the point using a pinpoint dab of white glue or clear nail polish. Another option is to attach the insect right to the pin with glue or nail polish. A third possibility is to put the pin through a special rectangular piece of cork and then attach the insect to the cork by pinning it with a tiny piece of wire called a "minutien." These supplies are available from Insect Museum Supply and other biological supply houses. The pinning methods are illustrated in Figure 7-24.

Fragile, large-winged insects might better be stored in

Methods of Pinning Small Insects

using a point   gluing to the pin

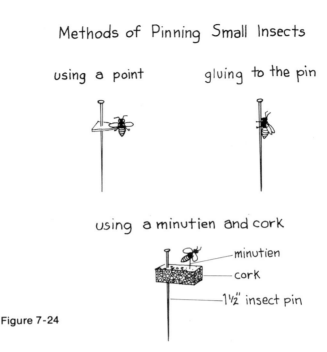

using a minutien and cork

— minutien

— cork

— 1½″ insect pin

Figure 7-24

an envelope of folded paper than on a pin. With long insects, such as walkingsticks or some large dragonflies, it is wise to use two pins to support the length of the body (see Figure 7-25).

Once pinned and labeled, the insects can be stored in boxes. "Insect Boxes," with a cork layer on the bottom and a catch to close them, are sold by the biological supply houses. For less formal collections, a cigar box or a corrugated cardboard box will work fine. If the bottom of your box does not already have a thick layer of some sort to stick the pin into, a ½-inch sheet of Styrofoam can be used. Tape a mothball to the side of the box to ward off insects like dermestid beetles and book lice, which make it their business to reduce the amount of debris in the world.

When insects are stored in alcohol (70 to 90 percent ethyl or 40 to 70 percent isopropyl), the labels go right into the storage jars rather than being taped to the outside (see Figure 7-26). Write with India ink. You can also dip the

Storing Large, Fragile Insects in a Folded Paper Envelope

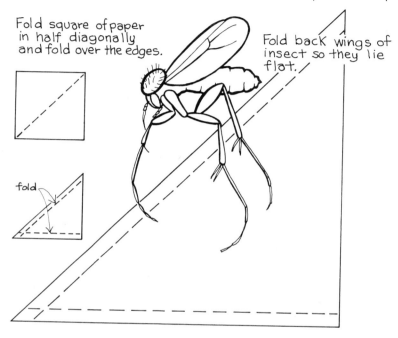

Fold square of paper in half diagonally and fold over the edges.

Fold back wings of insect so they lie flat.

fold

Figure 7-25

labels into vinegar to fix the ink before putting them into the alcohol.

For small or temporary collections, baby food or spice jars work fine. But for larger, long-term collections, where you must be concerned that the storage liquid does not evaporate, you may want to purchase special vials and set up a storage system that will not take up much room.

Straight-sided glass vials of various sizes can be ordered from the supply houses. Although the vials come with cork stoppers, it is better to stopper them with tight wads of cotton since the tannic acid in the corks can mix with the alcohol and acidify the solution. Other types of stoppers, such as rubber or neoprene, are also not recommended because they can react chemically with the alcohol and

Alcohol Storage System

bail — jar lid

rubber
gasket

glass-top canning jar
with metal bail and
rubber gasket

alcohol solution

label for
large jar

cotton wad
small vials filled with
alcohol solution
label

Figure 7-26

damage your specimens. Screw-cap vials tend to loosen in time so that the alcohol evaporates.

Of course, if a vial with a cotton stopper is left out in the air, the alcohol will evaporate in no time. That is why a number of small vials are stored together in larger jars which are also filled with alcohol. Glass-topped canning jars with a wire bail and rubber gasket are highly recommended, and plastic-lidded screw-top jars are also satisfactory. The larger jars should be checked periodically (every six months to a year) to make sure that the level of alcohol in them is high enough. Screw-top jars can be taped shut to further retard the evaporation process.

There is a diversity of opinion on the matter of adding a small amount of glycerin to the alcohol solution. On the positive side, the glycerin forms a protective coating over the specimens which prevents them from drying out if the alcohol evaporates. On the negative side, the glycerin forms a messy, slippery coating which can support the growth of mold. So take your choice! If you want to use glycerin, you can buy it in the drugstore where it is sold to treat chapped skin. Both ethyl and isopropyl alcohol are also sold in the drugstore as rubbing alcohols.

Marking Insects

Do you ever wonder if the insects you see in your garden day after day are the same ones—considering your home as theirs, protecting and patrolling it as you do, eating and sleeping there—or if there is a steady parade of transient insects in and out of the area? To help answer this question, which has value in addition to the rewards of philosophical speculation, you can mark some of the insects to help keep track of them.

Perhaps the best method of marking insects is to put spots on the thorax (or the elytra of beetles). You can use colored wax crayons applied with a hot blunt needle or artist's oil paints, dyes, lacquers, inks, or nail polish applied with a fine brush. You can vary the color and pattern so that individual insects can be recognized. To keep the insects still while they are being marked, first put them into the refrigerator where the cold will slow them down.

Ladybugs (family Coccinellidae) are a great favorite of biological control advocates since different species (over 4,000 species worldwide including 370 in North America) voraciously devour aphids, mealybugs, scales, whiteflies, and spider mites. With their life work so much to human liking, it is no wonder that humans have tried to domesticate them and to increase their numbers by gathering them up while they are in hibernation or by rearing them in mass numbers in controlled environments.

What's the result? The introduced beetles often come out of hibernation and instinctively fly away from the gardens they have been sent to, leaving the smaller native populations of ladybugs to eat some of the aphids and other pests as they have always done. The potential benefits of using large numbers of ladybugs as pest control agents have, however, kept researchers working away developing rearing and collection methods that would break this escape pattern. Why don't *you* become a judge of their success?

Buy some of the beetles offered as biological control agents. Mark them using one of the methods described below and then observe or collect (without harming) the ladybugs as you see them working in the garden. How many have the markings you put on them? How many do not and are, therefore, old residents?

"Mark, release, and recapture" programs can be used to estimate the total local population of an insect species as long as it is a type of insect that does not migrate in and out of the area. The system is called the Lincoln Index and was originally developed for use with small mammals. Its accuracy depends upon there being a stable population between the time of marking and of recapturing. With the sometimes very short life span of insects and with their potential for transiency, the stability of the population cannot be guaranteed and the results, therefore, should only be considered an approximation.

Collect a certain number of the insects, say 25, mark them and then release them. Then, from randomly chosen sampling areas around your experimental plot, collect with a net or trap the same species (or collect all insects that fall into your net or traps, but count only those of the species in question). Count the number of those captured that have the mark you put on them. With these figures, make the following computations:

$$\frac{\text{total number marked} \times \text{total number captured}}{\text{total number of marked insects recaptured}} = \text{total population estimate}$$

For example, if 25 insects were collected and marked and a total of 75 later captured, 5 of which had the mark on them, then:

$$\frac{25 \times 75}{5} = 375 \text{ population estimate.}$$

Experiments Involving Insects

The number of experiments you could do involving insects is endless. Virtually any statement in a gardening book or magazine addressing itself to the issue of pest management remains open to being tested under the particular set of conditions in *your* garden. Many of the recommended practices have been passed on as a sort of folklore and their effectiveness may never have been rigorously tested or examined to see *why* they seem to work.

Does spraying your plants with tobacco juice or ringing

them with ashes, for example, really ward off pests? (Which pests, off which plants, using how much of the repellent and how often?) How about a spray made of pureed insects in a water solution with a little bit of soap (so it sticks)? Lots of people say it works. Does it kill pests or just repel them? Does it only work when used to ward off the same insect as the type used in the spray mixture? Does it work because you are spreading around an insect disease or is there some other, more mysterious, reason for its charm?

Can butterflies really be fooled into laying eggs on strips of old flannel pajamas rather than on the leaves of cabbage plants? What about hiding the cabbage or brussels sprouts or broccoli in among other plants to camouflage them so that their insect enemies, normally attracted by their characteristic blue-gray color, cannot find them?

Working out a solution to any of these questions means, for a start, that you must know which of the many insects flying around are the ones causing problems with your plants. There are some other points to keep in mind as well. Your plots should be uniformly attractive to the insect in question. Of course that means they should be on equally fertile land, but it also means you should be aware of how close they are placed to a weedy border, hedgerow, or water source which could affect the size of the insect population. You will not be able to compare the effect of a spray or other treatment variable unless the baseline conditions are equal.

Insect behavior changes with the weather and with the time of day. It has to do, partly, with the barometric pressure, with the heating and drying powers of the sun, and with the effect of these factors on the flow of nectar in flowers. Also it has to do with light polarity, by which many insects navigate, which is at a minimum at noon and much stronger at dawn and dusk. And it probably also has to do with factors we can only guess at and could not begin to measure. The net result is that when you count insect numbers or observe their behavior, you will witness different phenomena depending on the hour of the day or night. So before settling into a routine of midmorning observations, when the insects in question may be sleeping in the shade, get out there at odd hours and see what is happening!

Just keep in mind that if you are comparing the number of pest insects in plots A and B, you should collect data from both plots at approximately the same time of day.

Try out different methods of collecting your data to see which is the most effective in your situation. Are you able to get the information you need by swinging your insect net at random or is it better to get down on your hands and knees and carefully examine the leaves and flowers of sample plants? With nonflying insects such as the larval and nymph stages, and the aphids and scales, counting numbers per unit area might be the best approach.

Finally, how intensive a control effort is needed to produce the desired results? Evaluate the yield of your crop, both how much there is and how good it is, to see the effect of the pest control measures. For further reading, see Chiang 1977; Clausen 1956; DeBach and Schlinger 1964; Reed and Webb 1975; Schwartz 1975, 1977; and Westcott 1960.

EARTHWORMS

Earthworms are perhaps the biggest and most famous of garden invertebrate animals. Unlike slugs, they are known for their good works. Their ability to ingest and break down organic matter is prodigious, and results in production of nutrient-rich castings. By burrowing through the soil, they introduce beneficial microflora and thoroughly mix organic matter with soil particles while increasing soil porosity.

It is generally conceded by organic gardeners that earthworms are great to have around. It might be interesting for you to do some experimenting to see if different conditions which you can create in your garden are conducive to increasing the earthworm population. Do you find as many earthworms in a chemically fertilized garden as you do in a compost-enriched garden? Does the type of compost or manure you use make a difference? How about the presence or absence of mulch? Or the use of a leaf or straw cover over your garden in the winter?

169

Earthworms are advertised and sold as a method of improving the soil. You might set up an experiment to see if such large-scale introduction of earthworms is beneficial, or if merely providing the right environment with enough organic matter for food does the trick in encouraging an earthworm population to stay alive and reproduce in your garden. Buy some of the advertised worms; introduce them to an isolated section of your garden and then, at intervals, sample from this area and from other areas of the garden to compare the earthworm populations. It would be interesting to see if, over time, there were significantly more earthworms in the area where they were introduced or if the population soon balanced out with that of the rest of the garden.

It may be that your garden is already supporting as many earthworms as it can under existing conditions and that the worms you introduce will not be able to compete with the established residents and will die off due to lack of food (or, vice versa, the oldtimers may not be able to survive the competitive pressures of the newcomers). When doing such an experiment, you should take your first samples *before* the purchased worms are introduced so that you have base-level population figures for future comparisons.

The lifestyles of the different species of earthworms vary. Not only are they found in very different habitats—some in gardens, some in sewage effluent, some along stream beds, some in manure piles—but their manner of living even within a garden differs. The large and common night crawler (*Lumbricus terrestris*) makes deep vertical tunnels, others make tunnels that are horizontal, others live in surface leaf litter. (As used here "litter" does not mean garbage, but refers to the layer of undecomposed organic material—leaves, seed coats, animal droppings, etc.—found on top of the mineral soil.) Obviously, where and how you sample will affect the type of worm you will find.

Sampling Methods

Since earthworms are irregularly distributed in the soil, it is better to take many small soil samples rather than a few large samples. A recommended size is 10 inches x 10 inches x 4 inches. With ten samples per treatment you can come reasonably close to finding the true population density of your plot.

Some species of earthworms become inactive when conditions are unfavorable. At these times they can be difficult to find. You can deal with this problem by doing sequential sampling so that your conclusions are not based just on the results of one sampling experience.

Hand Sorting

The most reliable method of finding earthworms is to dig a soil sample, put it in a large tray, and sort through it by hand. Doing this you should be able to find virtually all of the larger worms, including those in an inactive stage. However, you will probably overlook some specimens of the smaller species and of the immature worms. The major drawbacks to this method are that it is laborious and that digging can destroy some of the worms as well as the habitat.

Formaldehyde Extraction

A method of extracting worms from soil and surface litter using a formaldehyde solution was developed in the late 1950s (Raw 1959). The effectiveness of this method varies with soil temperature and moisture level and with how completely and rapidly the solution can penetrate the earthworm tunnels and drive out the worms. The effects differ depending on the soil type and the type of burrowing system. This method works better with surface-feeding and shallow-burrowing worms than it does in extracting very deep burrowers or those worms which make horizontal tunnels. Also, only active worms respond to the formaldehyde.

Because of the many factors which can introduce experimental error, formaldehyde extraction is best used as a comparative index rather than as a means of arriving at the total number or biomass of worms in an area. This sampling method is far less time-consuming than hand sorting, however, and using it does not disturb the habitat. At the recommended concentration, formaldehyde is not dangerous in your garden since it breaks down very rapidly.

The usual procedure is to sample an area 20 inches x 20 inches by slowly pouring on one gallon of solution so that it all seeps into the soil and does not run off. The solution is made by using one tablespoon of formalin for each gallon of water. Formalin is an aqueous solution of formaldehyde gas—generally available in a 40 percent solution[4]

Formalin is an irritant which drives the worms from the soil so you can pick them up as they emerge. The standard collection period is the ten minutes after pouring on the solution. A second and third application to the same sampling unit at ten minute intervals will increase your take. For the third application you can remove the top layer of soil before pouring on the solution so as to be able to reach deeper burrowing worms.

Heat Extraction

Using heat to drive worms from a soil sample into water is recommended when you are sampling soil with a dense mat of vegetation, as in a pasture or uncultivated field. Sorting through such a sample by hand would be nearly impossible. This is a good way to capture smaller worms which are likely to be overlooked while hand sorting, but heat extraction requires a bit of initial effort to set up and then several hours to extract each sample.

You will need to set up a small extraction tank as shown in Figure 7-27. Use a plastic baby bath or similar tub measuring approximately 20 inches on each side (the exact size is not critical). Support a wire mesh sheet 2 inches above the bottom of the tub and rest your soil sample on it. Fill the tub with water to a level halfway up the soil sample. On top of the tub rest two wooden battens and above this a hardboard sheet into which holes have been drilled so that you can screw in 14 60-watt light bulbs. The light bulbs should be about 1 inch above the soil sample and should remain on for three hours.

The idea is that the bulbs provide heat which warms up

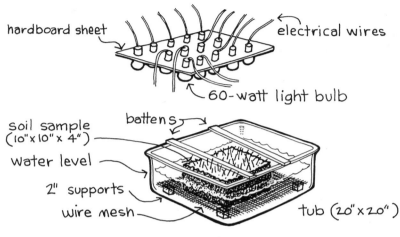

Heat Extraction Tank
(Adapted from Satchell 1971)

hardboard sheet

electrical wires

60-watt light bulb

soil sample (10" x 10" x 4")

battens

water level

2" supports

wire mesh

tub (20" x 20")

Figure 7-27

the soil, making it uncomfortable for the worms so they are driven into the surrounding water bath. They should be removed from the water immediately following the three-hour extraction period (Satchell 1969, 1971).

Preserving and Identifying Earthworms

At this point you can either simply count the number of worms found in each sampling unit or you can separate the different types of worms and try to identify them. A suggested method of preparing the worms for identification is to anesthetize them in a 50 percent solution of ethyl or isopropyl alcohol until they stop moving, then straighten them out by placing them between two plates of glass. After they die, replace the alcohol with 10 to 50 percent formalin which will harden them in position. The formalin should be changed after 24 hours and then again at weekly intervals until the solution stays clear. Formalin does a good job of retaining the original color of the worms. If they remain in the alcohol solution, they stay limp and eventually will turn a brownish color.

Definitive identification of earthworms can be quite difficult, often requiring the use of a microscope and dissection as well. The descriptions below mention a few field characteristics that can aid you in distinguishing between some of the worms you may find in your gardens, compost, or leaf litter. The information presented is quite general, and you should remember that in different sections of the country you may find different species of worms. More detailed reference sources are cited at the end of this chapter; those with keys to the identification of earthworms are marked with an asterisk.

Field Characteristics

The worms can be divided into two groups: the "lumbricine" group, which have their setae (short bristles) arranged in four rows of two each, and the "perichaetine" group, which have a ring of many setae all around each body segment. As a result these worms feel rough to the touch (see Figure 7-28). *Pheritima* is the only genus mentioned below that is in the latter group.

Diplocardia are common garden worms; some are quite large (up to 12 inches) but others are just half that size. The major way to differentiate members of this genus is that they are the only worms in the lumbricine group where the clitellum begins on or before the 15th body segment.

Eisenia: Eisenia foetida is very commonly found in manure and compost piles and is easy to recognize because of the purple-brown and buff banding of its body segments. The two colors alternate like rings down the length of the worm's body, which ranges from 1½ to 5 inches (usually less than 3 inches). The other species you may find is *Eisenia rosea*, a small worm 1 to 3 inches long and pale red or grayish in color. Its clitellum is often flared or bell-shaped in cross section.

Allolobophora: Allolobophora chlorotica is now considered to be the only species in this genus. It is 1¼ to 3 inches long and often a green color (sometimes yellow, pink, or gray) with a pink clitellum. It is found in a wide variety of habitats wherever the soil is wet with much organic matter.

Distinguishing Characteristics of Earthworms

Setae are difficult to see without a microscope, but you may be able to make out four longitudinal ridges down the length of the body of the worm. When the worms are wet, water stands out in beads on the setae.

setal arrangement of
lumbricine group of
earthworms, seen
in cross section

setal arrangement of
perichaetine group of
earthworms, seen in
cross section

The clitellum is a swelling around a few of the body segments of sexually mature worms. The type and placement of the clitellum are important features in earthworm identification.

The saddle
clitellum does
not completely encircle
the body segments.

The annular
clitellum goes
around the body
like an armband.

The flared
clitellum, found
just on Eisenia rosea, is
bell-shaped in cross section.

Figure 7-28

Aporrectodea previously were known as *Allolobophora* and that is how they are listed in older literature. They are shallow burrowers in garden and woodland soil, are rose or brown-red or pale gray in color, 2 to 8 inches long and are one of the groups easily extracted with the formalin method.

Dendrobaena: Dendrobaena octaedra are surface feeders found in leaf litter and in wet soil contaminated with sewage. They are not usually found in cultivated soils. They are ¾ to 1½ inches long, dark red to purple in color, and their posterior end is octagonal in shape when seen in cross section.

Dendrodrilus: Dendrodrilus rubidus was formerly classed with the *Dendrobaena*. It is from 1 to 3 inches long, is dark red and is found in gardens, fields, compost, and manure as well as in uncultivated areas.

Bimastos are found in a wide variety of habitats high in organic content. Most of the species are quite small (1 to 3 inches), but one species (*Bimastos longicinctus*) can get up to 6 inches in length. They are various shades of red and brown and are more common in warmer climates.

Octolasion: Octolasion cyaneum is from 2 to 7 inches and is blue-gray in color with the last four to five segments yellow and the front segments pink. The clitellum is red-orange. It is not very common in North America.

Octolasion tyrtaeum (Octolasion lacteum) is white, gray, blue or rose-pink with a pink or orange clitellum. Found in lawns and gardens as well as under logs and in decaying leaf mold and stream beds, it is from 1½ to 5 inches long.

Lumbricus: The four species in this genus all tend to be flattened dorso-ventrally (from top to bottom) in the body segments behind the clitellum. *Lumbricus terrestris* is the night crawler of fishing bait fame. It is brown-violet in color dorsally (top side) and yellow-orange ventrally (bottom side) and ranges from 4 to 12 inches in length. It can be differentiated from the large *Diplocardia*, the only other North American earthworm attaining its size, because its clitellum does not start until after the 30th body segment. It is a deep burrower in lawn and garden soil, coming to the surface at night and pulling leaves and other organic debris into its burrow, which often plug up the opening.

Lumbricus rubellus is 2 to 6 inches in length, ruddy brown or red-violet and iridescent dorsally, and pale yellow ventrally. It thrives in just about any habitat high in organic matter. *Lumbricus castaneus* is a small (1 to 2 inches), active, deep burrower, found 1 to 2 yards below surface when conditions are not favorable. It is a deeply pigmented dark red, chestnut or violet-brown and iridescent. *Lumbricus festivus* is a rarer member of the group. Thus far the only records of it in North America are from the Northeast where it has been found in pastures, dung, and leaves. It is an iridescent, ruddy brown color dorsally and light in color ventrally.

Pheritima: These worms have their setae in a ring all around each body segment so they feel rough to the touch. They are quick-moving and "snakelike," ranging from 3 to 8 inches. *Pheritima hupiensis*, which is the species you are most likely to come across in garden soils, is light green to greenish-buff with a pale gray underside and a milky or chocolate colored clitellum.

If you want to know more about earthworms, try reading some of these books and articles (an asterisk * indicates that the reference includes a key to species of worms): Causey 1961*; Edwards and Lofty 1972*; Reynolds 1972, 1977*; and Satchell 1955, 1967, 1969, 1971.

Notes

1. "Biological control is the suppression of the reproductive potential of organisms through the action of other organisms . . . natural control is the suppression of organisms unaided by man that may result from the effects of physical or biological factors." (Fisher 1960).

2. Animals (and plants as well) are classified according to a system that puts related members into the same groups, beginning with the premise that animals are more closely related to each other than they are to plants, fungi, or one-celled organisms. Thus all multicelled animals are placed in the animal kingdom. The levels of classification (called "taxons") get increasingly more specific until reaching the "species," which groups individuals structurally similar to one another and capable of interbreeding and producing fertile offspring. The major levels of classification are the kingdom, phylum, class, order, family, genus, and species. The nonsense phrase "King Philip Came Over From Germany" can help you keep this sequence straight.

The Mexican bean beetle, a very beautiful golden beetle with eight dark spots on each elytron (hardened fore wing), but a very serious garden pest, is classified as follows:

Animal Kingdom

Phylum Arthropoda (which includes crustaceans, millipedes, centipedes, horseshoe crabs, sea spiders, and arachnids, i.e., spiders and mites as well as insects

Class Insecta (containing 27 orders)

Order Coleoptera (beetles)

Family Coccinellidae (comprised mostly of the very bene-

ficial predators known as ladybugs or ladybird beetles)
  Genus *Epilachna*
  Species *varivestis*
Species are generally identified using the "binomial system" which includes both the genus and species (for example, *Epilachna varivestis*). It is always italicized or underlined when written. Often the name of the "author," the person who first described the organism in a scientific publication, follows the binomial. So the Mexican bean beetle is officially known as *Epilachna varivestis* Mulsant. These Latinized binomials are valuable for their worldwide uniformity, whereas common names often change within the space of a few miles.

3. Each time a larva sheds its skin or "molts," it grows a little and begins a new "instar."

4. This dilution is ¼ to ½ percent (0.25 to 0.50 percent) of 40 percent formalin.

8

Tilling the Soil

Whatever happened to the good old days, to the simple times when a person knew that the way to start a garden was to go out in the springtime and turn over the soil? Now everything is so much more confusing.

On the one hand, the Biodynamic/French Intensive method (Jeavons 1974) tells us to dig twice as deeply as we did before. On the other hand, folks are suggesting that we shouldn't turn over the soil at all. That, you may think, is a strange idea, but actually it is the way that plants have always managed it on their own—with no plowing or cultivating, with other plants growing up haphazardly around them, and with the remains of last year's plants crumpled at their feet. Seeds dropped onto the ground, and the ones best suited to the environment survived. The pulsing of living things kept the soil loose and airy with rootlets pushing, earthworms burrowing, and lots of smaller creatures making their way through the earth. Plant debris and the tangle of roots moderated the effects of wind and water so that erosion was hardly a thought and even drought was not usually a problem.

So it went on for eons, until people came and wanted to grow crops of special use to them instead of the plants which came up of their own accord. With this began the practice of clearing land for planting. Various cultivating methods developed. The plow was invented in many forms, in many parts of the world. It was used to break up sod and bury weed growth so that the planted seeds would have a chance to grow.

According to Edward H. Faulkner, author of *Plowman's Folly* (1943), the plow also accelerated the processes of soil depletion and erosion. By plowing-under plant remains each season, a layer of organic matter was helplessly sandwiched between the soil on top and the subsoil. Organic matter absorbs moisture like a sponge and without this spongy layer on top, the soil dried out. The force of pouring rain splashing on the bare ground dislodged particles and washed them away. When the wind blew, the soil was carried away with it, creating dust storms.

Faulkner's book created quite some turbulence itself, coming out as it did on the heels of the major dust storms of the mid-1930s. The Western Plains were coated with dust as much as 6 inches deep and huge dust clouds lumbered across the country until eventually they rode out over the Atlantic Ocean.

The storms were the result of land mismanagement. Large areas that had been pasture were plowed up and used for row crops. This worked well enough for a few years, especially when the amount of rainfall was higher than usual. Then when the rain returned to its normal low level, the plowed lands, now without a grassy cover, became parched and dusty from exposure to the sun and wind.

After looking at the following figures on soil erosion in this country, you may be interested in trying out some of the methods of no-plow agriculture which we will be talking about in the rest of this chapter.

By 1940 some 200 million acres in the United States that had been farmed in the past could no longer be used for agriculture due to the erosion of the topsoil. The average loss of topsoil from agricultural land is 12 tons per acre per year. This is replenished at the much slower average rate of 1.5 tons per acre per year as minerals break off from the bedrock and organic matter is deposited from the wastes of plants and animals. One-and-a-half tons translates into about 1 inch of new topsoil each hundred years. It is a slow process (see Pimentel et al. 1976).

Winds account for about one-fourth of the erosion, while water runoff is responsible for the rest. You might think that wind is the adversary in arid regions and water is the foe where there is a lot of rain, but that is not exactly the case. In areas where rain rarely falls, it is often torrential when it finally does come down. Parched soils with sparse vegetative cover are unable to absorb the sudden deluge of water, so the rain splashes away, carrying soil particles with it. Deep gullies are visible evidence of this erosion, but greater damage is actually done by the less obvious "rill and sheet" erosion which washes thin layers of soil from even the gentlest of slopes. You may not notice the damage until crops at the top of a hill do poorly or until the soil color appears to differ along the slope, depending on how much of the topsoil has been carried away.

Soils fall victim to the forces of erosion at different rates, depending on a number of factors: the material from which the soil is made; the velocity of the winds that blow on it; the amount of rain that falls; how hard and at what time of year it falls; the slope of the land and the length of the slope; and the plants that are grown on it.

Where row crops are planted year after year, the losses are greatest. When they are rotated with other crops, the losses are somewhat less, but still more than when the small grains—oats, wheat or barley—are grown. Ground covers protect the soil—the best ground covers are plants with an intricate tangle of roots in addition to a dense surface growth, such as the clovers, alfalfas, and grassy sods. Soil losses are least from undisturbed forest lands (see Brady 1974, Foth 1978, Pimentel et al. 1976, Townsend 1973, and Van Vliet, Wall and Dickonson 1976).

This message has not fallen on deaf ears. Many acres that were previously planted in row crops have been returned to pasture or woodlands. Many farmers are now growing their corn by low-tillage methods, planting right into the stubble left from the previous year's growth or into the sod following a rotation. This is not just the experimentation of a few farmers seeking alternatives. Half the corn planted in the state of Maryland in 1973 was grown with low-tillage methods according to Bandel et al. 1975.

Gardeners can also learn a lesson from the dust storms. Vegetables are row crops, and the soil they are grown on is subject to erosion. So maybe we should take a look at the good points and also at the drawbacks of low-tillage methods of cultivation.

There must, certainly, be some problems when the soil is not plowed, otherwise people would not have started to use a plow in the first place. The problem of course is the weeds. If you are not going to plow them under, how are you going to get rid of them?

In *Plowman's Folly* Faulkner suggests that instead of plowing the weeds and stubble under they be disked into the top layer of soil. This would leave what he calls a "trashy" layer of organic material on the surface to protect the soil from the ravages of wind and rain. Planting would be done with a dibble stick or with a wheel with lugs attached at intervals equal to the desired distance between seeds (see Figure 8-1). Faulkner acknowledges that in the first few years of working an area the weeds may be so overwhelming that plowing may be necessary. But others are finding that plowing is not necessary, even in the beginning.

Herm and Miriam Bieling are friends of mine here in upstate New York. Their big and bountiful hillside garden is something to boast of. A few years ago they extended their garden into an old field that had long been left alone and which was quite overgrown. They experimented to see if it

Tools for Low—Tillage
Methods of Cultivation

dibble stick

wheel with lugs attached which can be used for planting

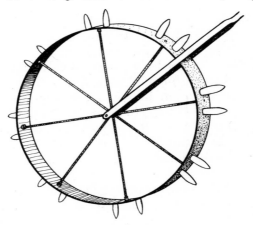

Figure 8-1

would be possible to start using the land without even turning over the soil. To tame the wild growth Herm and Miriam
stamped down the weeds and then covered that area with a
leaf mulch. Mulches block out the sun's rays and this keeps
down the weeds while also protecting the soil from the
eroding forces of wind and rain.

Herm planted potatoes that first year because they are
able to push up through the mulch. He has found that it does

not matter if the mulch is put on the previous fall or right at planting time. In fact he waited until he laid down the seed potatoes before mulching. He finds that the key lies in trampling down the weeds rather than mowing them or pulling them out. (Cutting a weed is like pinching back the straggly ends of your houseplants; it forces vigorous new growth from the side buds.)

Once their crops are established, the Bielings do not mind if some weeds push back up through the mulch. There is enough ground-water here to provide moisture for all plants without causing undue competition between them. Herm and Miriam find that the weeds are, in fact, helpful because they act as a "living mulch," keeping the soil in place when the strong winds blow down the valley. If the weeds become too overwhelming, the Bielings just tramp them down.

Of a like mind with regard to the tramping vs. mowing of weeds was the somewhat famous farmer-researcher, Louis Bromfield, who wrote several books elaborating on his life and work at Malabar Farm in Ohio (1976). Bromfield found that when he planted corn into a living mulch of alfalfa or clover, the corn did better if the cover crop had not just been mowed. If left alone, the legume would have nearly completed its growth for the season by the time the corn was planted. But if it were mowed, it would have another growth spurt and would be strong competition for the little corn seedlings.

Bromfield did not actually plant the corn directly into the sod, but plowed strips 10 inches wide and planted into these rows. This way he was able to use standard farm machinery to do the planting and harvesting. He experimented with this system for five years and found that when there was moisture stress early in the season, the perennial sod with its long roots was able to prosper while the corn seedlings could not get a foothold and the crop failed. In other years, when there was adequate early moisture, the corn started up vigorously and soon shaded out and killed the legumes, grasses, and any weeds that may have started up.

Even though he saved 80 percent in time, labor, and gasoline by not having to do as much work in the field,

Box 8-1: Low-Tillage in the Tropics

Louis Bromfield was inspired to do his intercropping experiments when he saw corn grown very successfully in the midst of a dense stand of weeds in the Amazon Jungle of Brazil. The weeds formed a "living mulch" for the corn that did not restrict its growth or productivity. The heavy tropical rainfall accounts for lush foliar growth, but also rapidly leaches nutrients out of the soil where ground is cleared for cultivation. Without a mulch, farmlands in tropical rain forests remain productive for only a very few years.

High-climbing weeds and tall grasses make a rather unpredictable mulch, however, which can choke out smaller and less vigorous crops than corn. But by planting a low-growing cover crop, the soil is protected and the growth of other weeds inhibited.

This system of soil management is being developed at the International Institute of Tropical Agriculture in southern Nigeria where the amount of rainfall can be as much as in the Amazon Jungle. The "living mulch" that has been found to be the most successful there is *Desmodium triflorium* FC, a low-lying, nonclimbing relative of the tick-trefoils found in this country. It is easily propagated, fights off other weedy growth and is leguminous, so that it adds nitrogen to the soil.

An automatic planter based on the idea of the dibble stick or jab planter has been developed by the researchers in Nigeria. A disk first slices through the mulch; then two disks in a V-formation create a furrow; then the planter drops in seeds to the desired depth.

According to Dr. Bede N. Okigbo, excellent crops of corn, sorghum, cowpea, pigeon pea, upland rice and tomato have all been produced using this method of low-tillage agriculture (see Okigbo 1977).

Bromfield did not wholeheartedly recommend this as a tillage system for corn. He felt it was a gamble which only paid off when the weather cooperated. Perhaps with a different cover crop or a different ratio of sod to corn or in an area where the rainfall is more predictable, the system would be more dependable. These are some of the very problems now being investigated at the Organic Gardening and Farming Research Center in Maxatawny, Pennsylvania.

You might wonder why there should still be so many unsolved questions when many farmers are already using low-tillage methods successfully. It is because most farmers are solving the problem of the weeds by using herbicides on the fields before planting. This not only introduces still more poisons into the agricultural system, but also eliminates the energy savings that could be realized by not doing all that plowing and cultivating. And as Louis Bromfield found out, these can be considerable.

Those of you who do not use power machinery would also be saving—especially your back, legs, and arms—since you would not be doing as much lifting, turning, and weeding of the soil. This advantage alone may make low-tillage agriculture very attractive, even if soil erosion is not a problem in your garden. In adapting this system to your gardening regime, there are many points you can consider, each of which could spin off an endless number of experimental possibilities.

A mulch on the ground, for instance, is known to reduce the leaching of nutrients, keep the soil surface more moist, and alter the microclimate near the ground. That microclimate—the temperature and relative humidity affecting your plants—is not the same as what you are experiencing towering up there above the vegetables. An experiment measuring soil and air temperatures and relative humidity at various heights in gardens with and without a mulch would certainly give you insight to the change in conditions caused by a ground cover (see Geiger 1965).

As was pointed out by some of the researchers who had used them, living mulches—whether they be "weeds" or one of the selected cover crops—can cause a problem by competing for moisture and nutrients and thus reduce the productivity of your vegetable crop. The magnitude of the problem depends on several factors. One factor, the amount of precipitation, is environmental, but the others can be altered and adjusted with experimentation. They include the type of living mulch, the crop(s) you are growing, the density of each of them, and your method of seeding—whether it be into plowed rows or directly into the mulch.

The potential problems with living mulches can be avoided by using mulches of decaying organic matter. But the living mulch may also have certain other advantages. As a living plant it can, after all, be productive in its own right. Clippings can be used as material for the compost pile, as more mulch, or even as animal feed. If it is a legume, as many of the recommended cover crops are, consider the value of the nitrogen it contributes to the soil via the nitrogen-fixing bacteria living in nodules on its roots.

Many legumes, including some of the clovers and alfalfa, are among the plants most noted as nectar sources for honeybees. Thus, if there are bee hives in your area, a honey yield would be still another bonus from the living mulch. Check with a beekeeper to find out which plants are honey plants or look in a reference such as *Honey Plants Manual* (Lovell 1956) which is available from the beekeepers' supply houses.

You could conduct quite an interesting experiment evaluating just how many different ways a living mulch can be utilized. To compute the total productivity of a field grown with a living mulch you could, for example, add the yield of the main crop to that of the hay from the clippings to that of the honey and then also include the value of the fertilizer that did *not* have to be applied because of the nitrogen-fixing bacteria. For comparison, compute the yield of the same crop grown alone in a field of comparable quality. The comparison could be in monetary or caloric terms. (See Chapter 6.)

The ultimate way to utilize a cover crop and at the same time to make optimum use of the space available to you is to grow an edible living mulch. In my garden the low-lying "weeds" purslane and chickweed tend to wind about covering all the bare spots. They taste good and are nutritious and also confer the advantages (and disadvantages) of a living mulch. If these or similar plants cover your garden, you could set up an experiment comparing the productivity of

(Continued on page 192)

Box 8-2: Ideas for Experiments

THE "ORGANIC SANDWICH"

Dig a hole 2 feet deep in an uncultivated field and another in a field that has been plowed for a number of years. The sides of each hole should be vertical and cleanly cut so that you can see a "profile" of the soil layers. Do you see the "organic sandwich" that Edward H. Faulkner talked about in *Plowman's Folly*? (It should appear as a dark layer several inches below a layer of lighter soil in the plowed field.) According to his theory, the organic matter is sandwiched in under the plowed soil. In an uncultivated field the organic matter is in the top layer of soil.

RAINWATCH

During a rainstorm, watch the raindrops as they hit the ground to see if the water soaks in or if it rebounds. If the water does bounce up again after striking the ground, does it carry soil particles with it? Make this observation during rainstorms of various intensities and on bare ground, mulched gardens, soil with a ground cover, soil with a high organic content, etc.

Watch the water runoff from fields of different slopes and with different ground covers. If the runoff from your garden is not crystal clear, you are witnessing the process of soil erosion and had better go and do some more experimenting to develop a better tillage system.

COMPARING SOIL MANAGEMENT SYSTEMS

Compare several tillage systems: perhaps the one you have been using compared with the French Intensive method and with one or more low-tillage methods. Among the possible low-tillage methods are the following:

1. Using a mulch of decaying organic matter (leaves, straw, newspapers, etc.), spread over unplowed soil. Weeds may be dealt with by trampling them down or

mowing. Seeds can be planted with some type of dibble stick or by pushing the mulch aside.

2. Plant a low-lying "living mulch" and allow it to get established before planting crops directly into it.

3. Leave last year's stubble and plant debris and plant into it, with or without first disking or hoeing the organic matter into the top layers of soil.

4. Plant a "living mulch" and allow it to get established before plowing up strips and then plant crops into those rows.

Before incorporating any of these unfamiliar tillage systems into an experiment, you ought to try them out for a season so that you can become familiar with them and adapt and refine them as you see fit. This type of experiment is most worthwhile when continued for a number of years so that the effects of the soil management systems on the health of the soil can really be evaluated. The experimental design presented in Figures 8-2 and 8-3 is adapted from an experiment comparing "The Effect of Several Soil Management Systems on Soil Parameters and on the Productivity of Crops" (Eggert 1977).

In that experiment the French Intensive method was compared with two organic and two commercial systems of planting and soil management. The experiment was replicated five times so there was a total of 25 plots, each 4 feet by 25 feet. No low-tillage methods were included in the experiment. The size and number of plots that you use and the management systems that you evaluate are up to you and depend in part on the time and space available, but you can use Eggert's plan as a guide.

The experiment was laid out in a Latin square. Latin square designs are intended for use with from four to eight different treatments, so if you are just comparing two or three management systems, you should use a randomized block design.

Eggert prepared the French Intensive plots by digging poultry manure compost in to a depth of at least 18 inches and applying it at a rate of 1 cubic yard/100 square feet, which was

(Continued)

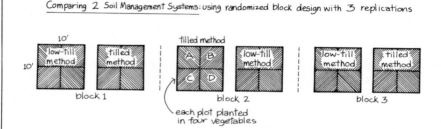

Figure 8-2

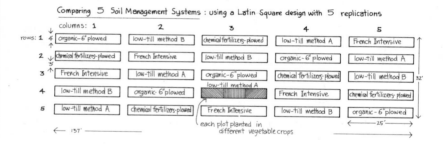

Figure 8-3

the size of a plot. Rock phosphate was applied at a rate of 12,000 pounds/acre which works out to about 30 pounds/plot. The same additives were used for the organic system, but they were worked into the soil to a depth of about 6 inches using a roto-hoe.

Before beginning the experiment, be certain that your plots are on soil of equal fertility. It would be helpful to have a complete soil analysis done before you begin so that you can compare the initial nutrient level with that shown by later analyses done after the management systems have been in effect for awhile.

An experiment like this can be evaluated in many ways. Soil erosion itself is a difficult quantity to measure, but the health of the soil can be measured by doing soil and plant nutrient analyses (see Chapter 3). Plant size and yield and the amount of insect and disease damage all reflect upon the success of a soil management system. If the attractiveness of your garden is important to you, you might also rate the plots according to that quality (rating systems are discussed in Chapter 9).

FERTILIZING WITH NO-PLOW AGRICULTURE

Since you will not be tilling, you will need to develop a method for applying and spreading fertilizer and compost that does not involve turning over the soil.

Since many of the suggested ground covers are legumes (and therefore have nodules of nitrogen-fixing bacteria on their roots), the need for additional nitrogen fertilization may be reduced. Set up an experiment comparing plots that are planted in the same crop and managed in the same way—with the exception of the amount of nitrogen-rich fertilizer added to each. Nutrients from an organic source are released slowly, so continue the experiments over several years.

Watch for signs of nutrient deficiency (see Sprague 1964) and also compare yields from the different plots.

INSECTS

Compare the magnitude of insect problems in plots with and without mulch or plant stubble. Many pest insects overwinter in the plant remains of the previous year's crop so that they are all ready for the new crop the following year. People who have used low-tillage methods have sometimes mentioned the increased problem they have with pests as a drawback to the system.

Plots can be compared by evaluating the amount of dam-

(Continued)

age done to the plants (you can evaluate plant vigor, productivity, percentage of the plant that is blemished, etc.) or by counting the number of pest insects that are collected. The same method(s) of counting and collecting should be used on all the plots. (For ways to collect and trap insects, see Chapter 7.)

Look also at the overall insect community in each of the plots. Is there more diversity of insect species in some of the plots? Differentiate between the helpful insects (the predators, the parasitoids, the pollinators) and the plant-eating pest insects. Figure out the relative proportion of the helpful and pest insects.

your main crop in plots where the "weed" cover is allowed to grow unhindered, is pulled out regularly or, perhaps, smothered with a mulch of leaves or straw.

If there is no significant difference in yield of the main crop (for an explanation of "significant difference," see Chapter 9), then you can consider the chickweed, purslane, or whatever as an edible bonus. If, however, the plots with the ground cover produce significantly less, you will have to make a decision about which crop is more important to you and reduce the density of the other accordingly.

Generally, with interplanted crops only 60 to 80 percent as much space is needed to produce as much as the same crops planted separately (Crookston 1977). This is because the two plants make different demands on the environment, so that the competition between them (interplant competition) is less than that between plants of the same type (intraplant competition). As a result, the plantings can be closer. Just how close is a matter for experimentation.

Many of the ideas that have come up in this chapter are good starting points for meaningful experimentation. Don't rush about completely changing everything you have done in the past without first doing some experimenting to see what works well in your garden or on your farm. As you try these different systems, weigh the good points against the bad, keeping in mind their long-term implications and effects on the soil and energy use.

PART III

EVALUATING YOUR RESEARCH

9

Collecting Data and Evaluating Your Experiment

Sometime during the course of your experiment, you will want to collect data and then to evaluate your results. To show you what is involved with these processes, let us set up, carry out, and analyze a hypothetical experiment in which three planting densities of peppers are compared.

PLANNING AND CARRYING OUT A HYPOTHETICAL EXPERIMENT

Step one is to have a clear idea of what you hope to find out by doing the experiment. In this case, I want to find out which planting arrangement to use; whether I can get a better yield from my plot of peppers by setting the plots closer together than the recommended density.

Step two is to decide what planting treatments to use. Each treatment should serve a purpose. The treatments should be different enough from one another so that if, in fact, it does matter whether one procedure is used rather than another, the results will reflect that difference.

For the experiment shown in Figure 9-1, I will plant one plot in the density recommended in the seed catalogs: 18 inches apart in rows 30 inches apart (shown in "Treatment B" below). Since I do my weeding and harvesting by hand, I wonder if spacing the rows 30 inches apart is necessary. If only 18 inches is needed between plants within the rows, then maybe 18 inches between rows is also sufficient. This arrangement is shown in "Treatment A." Lastly, I will have another treatment with just about the same planting density as in "Treatment A," but the plants will be arranged differently. They will be planted every 12 inches in rows 30 inches apart, as in "Treatment C." I expect the results from this treatment to indicate whether density or planting arrangement has the greater effect on yield.

Step three is to decide upon an experimental design. Since the pepper-density experiment is a field experiment with just three treatments, the randomized complete block design is the most appropriate. Next, I will decide on the number of replications and plot size, depending on the space and resources available and on the requirements of the experiment. Six by eight feet is about as small as the

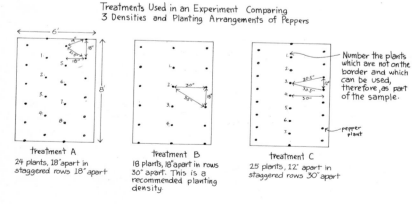

Treatments Used in an Experiment Comparing
3 Densities and Planting Arrangements of Peppers

treatment A
24 plants, 18˝ apart in staggered rows 18˝ apart

treatment B
18 plants, 18˝ apart in rows 30˝ apart. This is a recommended planting density.

treatment C
25 plants, 12˝ apart in staggered rows 30˝ apart

Number the plants which are not on the border and which can be used, therefore, as part of the sample.

pepper plant

Figure 9-1

plots can be for the pepper-density experiment because there are 2½ feet between rows and at least three rows are needed in order to sample properly due to the "border effect." The layout of this experiment and the randomization of the treatments are shown in Figure 9-2.

Step four is to figure out the materials needed for the experiment. All that I need for this experiment are pepper plants. To find out how many plants are required, I multiply the number needed for each treatment by four, the number of replications.

$$
\begin{array}{lrcl}
\text{A:} & 24 \times 4 & = & 96 \\
\text{B:} & 18 \times 4 & = & 72 \\
\text{C:} & 25 \times 4 & = & 100 \\
\hline
\text{Total:} & & & 268
\end{array}
$$

This totals quite a few pepper plants. I realize I should plan to purchase the plants I need rather than try to grow my own from seed. To make certain that I can get this many seedlings of the same variety started at the same time in the same growing medium and cared for in the same way, I will contact a greenhouse far in advance so that the growers can prepare this special order. In fact, I will order extra seedlings to be sure that I will have 268 of approximately equal vitality, with a reserve in case some do not survive the transplanting.

Step five is to decide which data to collect. Since I hope to find out which of the three planting arrangements is best, I should collect information on all factors which have an impact on determining what "best" is. Obviously I need to consider the yield from each plot, but that is not all. I must also consider the cost of the plants in relation to the value of the pepper crop. Since I need to purchase additional plants for the higher density plots, the extra cost must be covered by producing more peppers. There are also factors of quality: is one plot significantly easier or more difficult to care for; are there significant differences in the amount of insect or disease damage; or does the taste or appearance of the peppers vary significantly between treatments?

Step six is to consider how to collect the data. Should I

Plots for the Pepper-Density Experiment Laid Out in a Randomized
Block Design Showing 3 Treatments (A, B, C) with 4 Replications (blocks)

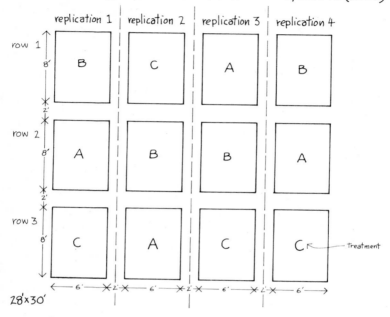

28'x30'

The blocks need not be located side by side as shown here. In fact, each replication can be located in a different garden.

To decide which treatment goes in which plot, write A, B, and C on 3 slips of paper. Mix up the papers, then choose 1 at a time, without knowing what is written on it. B was written on the first slip of paper chosen in this randomization so treatment B goes into the first plot of the first replication. Choose another slip of paper from the 2 remaining. In this case A was chosen, so treatment A goes into the second plot and treatment C into the third.

Now mix up the 3 papers again and choose the order for the second replication and then for the third and fourth.

Figure 9-2

collect it from all the experimental material or from some of it? This depends on the type of data and on the type of experiment.

Let's look at sampling methods used for different kinds of experiments and then discuss the particular procedures to be followed in the pepper-density experiment.

SAMPLING

What's a Sample?

With greenhouse and laboratory experiments or with those involving animals as sample units, you do not have to contend with the "border effect"; thus, you can use any of the individuals as part of your sample. With field experiments, however, it is probable that conditions differ along the edge of a plot. Therefore data should not be collected from plants or soil around plot borders.

With some experiments data collection is done simply by gathering information from the entire experimental population (excluding border plants). This would be the case if you were comparing the yields of two varieties of a crop grown on small plots. It would not serve any purpose to subdivide the plant population into sample units. Collecting data from the entire plot gives the most accurate information about your treatment population, but sometimes it can be inconvenient or impossible to gather material in this way.

Some measurements are too time-consuming or costly to be taken from more than a few plants in each plot. If you were measuring leaf size by the method of counting squares, for example, you could not possibly have the time to measure *all* the leaves. Or if you were having a nutrient analysis done in a laboratory, you probably could not afford to analyze each and every one of the plants.

There are also situations in which it would not be possible to gather data from the entire population. For instance, many populations studied in agricultural experiments are infinite in size. Or in a case where you were measuring the growth rate of a vegetable like turnips, you could not pick all your turnips to weigh them in August and then expect to see how much they had grown by September!

How Large a Sample?

In these cases where gathering data from the entire population is impossible, the accepted procedure is to take a sample from the treatment population. It is hard to tell you exactly how large the sample should be. It should contain a sufficient number of specimens to adequately represent the diversity of the treatment population. As discussed earlier (Chapter 3), some plant species show more variability between individuals than others because of differences in the way plants reproduce. These more variable plants require a larger number of sampling units so that the sample mean or average can be relied upon to approximate the mean of the entire population. Small plots must be sampled more intensively than large plots because the factor of importance is the absolute number of sample units, not the proportion of the experimental population which is represented.

Samples from each plot should be made up of the same number of sample units. This is so the "sampling error"—the amount that a sample average differs from a population average—is the same for all treatments. Sampling error decreases with an increased number of sampling units. Consistency in the size of the sampling error for all treatments is necessary in order to avoid complex adjustments in the statistical analysis of your work.

In choosing the number of sampling units, it is wise to remember that experimental results become more precise with a larger number of replications. Thus if your resources are limited in any way—whether by space, materials, time, or energy—it is best to limit the size of your plots or the size of your sample in order to be able to increase the *number* of samples by increasing the number of replications.

Sampling Methods

With carefully chosen sampling units, your sample data can come quite close to accurately representing the average conditions of the entire experimental population. It is important, however, that you choose your sampling units *before* it is time to collect the data. If you do not, it is tempting to allow your subjective opinions to influence the choice of a sample. Even though you may try to choose just "average-looking" sampling units, your idea of what is "average" is likely to be biased. Also, by trying to pick just "average-looking" plants, you will probably underestimate the diversity of the population. To compare one treatment with another, it is important that you are aware of the full range of possibilities for the experimental population.

Random Sampling

Instead of choosing sampling units by "eyeballing," you should use either a "random sampling" or a "systematic sampling" method. For the pepper-density experiment I will use random sampling. The number of plants I can sample from is limited by the number which are not border plants. In Treatment B there are only four plants in the interior of the plot, so I will use four sampling units from each of the plots. To decide which four plants to use, I have numbered the nonborder plants, as shown in Figure 9-1. I will randomly choose four plants from each plot by writing these numbers on slips of paper, mixing up the papers and pulling four from the pile—going through this process separately for each plot.

With larger plots you can use the Table of Random Digits, which is shown in Chapter 3, to choose the sampling units (see Figure 9-3). Number each plant (or plant location) and label it at planting time. Also draw a diagram of the arrangement. If you want to pick ten sampling units from 100 plants, arbitrarily choose two columns from the Table of Random Digits. By reading the two columns together you will have all of the two-digit numbers to choose from. Go down the list. The first ten numbers that match up with available plants will be your sampling units.

When you broadcast seeds or plant in beds rather than in rows, you can partition the plot into subplots (groups of plants within a designated area) from which to draw your sampling units (see Figure 9-4). Then you gather your data from a subplot instead of an individual plant. This method is used especially for experiments with small grains.

Choosing Sampling Units Using
the Table of Random Digits

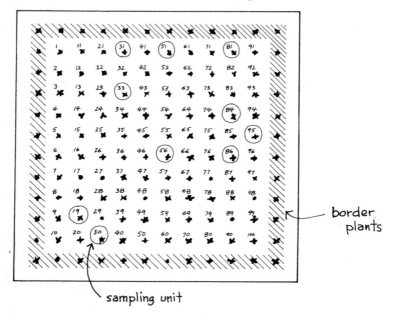

sampling unit

border
plants

Figure 9-3

This shows a plot of amaranth with 144 plants. The plants around the border are not counted. The 100 plants in the interior of the plot are numbered. Using columns 4 and 5 from the table of random digits in Chapter 3, count off the first 10 pairs of digits:

1) 31   6) 81
2) 33   7) 51
3) 86   8) 84
4) 56   9) 19
5) 95   10) 95

Since "95" appears twice, we go on and use the next pair of digits, "30," as our tenth sampling unit.

Random sampling works well with annual crops planted in garden or field-size plots where the plants easily can be numbered and labeled at planting time. It is less satisfactory when used over large areas (such as woodlands), because it does not guarantee an even distribution of sampling units from all over the plot.

Systematic Sampling

The weaknesses of random sampling are the strengths of systematic sampling. Complete randomness is sacrificed for maximum dispersion of sampling units, making it well suited for surveys over large areas. When you do a study along a transect line, as described in Chapter 3, you are sampling systematically.

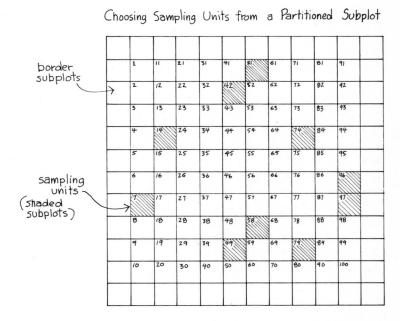

Choosing Sampling Units from a Partitioned Subplot

Using columns 7 and 8 of the Table of Random Digits, the sampling units are subplots 58, 97, 42, 7, 49, 14, 96, 51, 74 and 79.

Figure 9-4

Systematic Sampling from a Designated Area of a Plot

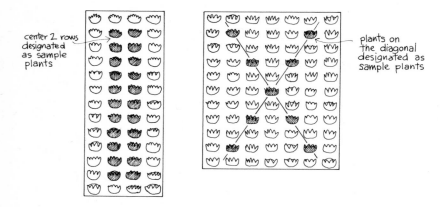

center 2 rows designated as sample plants

plants on the diagonal designated as sample plants

Figure 9-5

Start at a randomly chosen point on your plot and measure off a fixed distance or count off a fixed number of
plants, then take a sample. Repeat this process until you
have covered the entire area to be sampled. You must be
careful that the sampling intervals do not coincide with any
geographical factors, as would be the case if you sampled
every tenth plant in the plots shown in Figures 9-3 and 9-4.

Another method of systematic sampling used very commonly with small experimental plots is that of designating
an area within the plot as your sampling area. Researchers
often sample from all the plants in the center two rows of
their plots or from all the plants along the diagonal center of
the plot. These sampling arrangements are illustrated in
Figure 9-5.

What to Look For in Your Samples

After completing step six—choosing the sample—go on
to step seven. **Step seven is to decide what observations**

need to be made for each sampling unit. This depends on what information is being sought.

With any data collection you must first determine what it is you ultimately want to know and then what raw information must be compiled to get your answer. In most cases you can employ any of several strategies. The "Methods and Materials" section of published research papers may be helpful in describing the techniques used by other researchers in collecting data.

Destructive and Nondestructive Sampling

Your sampling technique may be either "destructive" or "nondestructive." Destructive sampling involves removing all or part of a plant (or catching an insect) so that its growth is disturbed or terminated. Sampling destructively does not reflect negatively on your personality type. In fact, for some types of analyses, it is the only way to get at the information. To find out the weight of a carrot, for example, you must pick the plant.

When you must do destructive sampling during the course of the growing season, you should be aware of the effect it has on the surrounding plants. (Midseason destructive sampling is necessary, for example, if you are to check root crops for insect damage or growth rate.) The remaining plants now may have less competition for nutrients, moisture, or sunlight, but they may also have had their root systems disturbed by the uprooting of one of their neighbors. Due to these disruptive effects, midseason destructive sampling is often restricted to one section of a plot, while later sampling is done in another section (see Figure 9-6).

Another problem with destructive sampling is that you can never know how the plant which you picked would have turned out had it been left to grow. If, for example, you are measuring plant hardiness by picking and weighing sample plants, it will forever be unknown if the heaviest seedlings early in the season would have turned out to be the most productive plants.

Destructive sampling can be avoided in collecting much of the data required by backyard researchers. Other

Limiting Destructive Sampling to Sections of a Plot

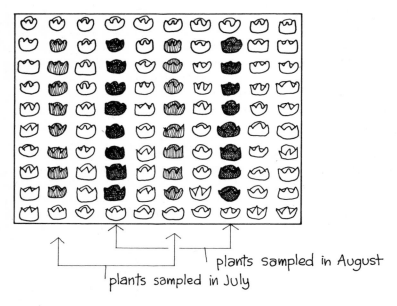

plants sampled in August

plants sampled in July

Figure 9-6

methods can often be used to gather the same information. Rather than weighing plants as a yardstick of their hardiness, you can, for example, measure their height and estimate their surface area.

Rating

Samples can also be "rated" on a judgment scale rather than measured in inches or in pounds. With rating you can simultaneously assess several features, such as girth, height, and color, to come up with an overall characterization of plant vigor. Rating is a good way to measure insect or disease damage, plant attractiveness, or the taste of a plant. Rather than using words to make your field observations, you can translate your notes into numerical terms using a rating scale.

To get back to the pepper-density experiment, I can

Box 9-1: Rating the Intensity of an Aphid Infestation

This rating scale was used to measure the intensity of an aphid infestation on kale. The kale was planted alone and interplanted with garlic in two different proportions to give a total of three treatments. The purpose was to see if the potent odor of the herb had an effect on reducing the number of aphids.

Make assessments by carefully looking at both sides of three leaves from each sample unit of kale. Use green leaves, one from the top, one from the middle, and one from the bottom of the plant. Look also at the junction of the leaves and the main stem of the plant. Use a 10x magnifier.

1. no infestation on any leaf

2. low-level infestation (fewer than 10 aphids) on one leaf; none on others

3. low-level infestation on two or three leaves

4. moderate infestation (10 to 30 aphids) on one leaf

5. moderate infestation on two or three leaves

6. heavy infestation on one leaf (more than 30 aphids)

7. heavy infestation on two or three leaves or a very heavy infestation (more than 60 aphids) on one leaf

---

rate how easy or difficult it is to work in plots planted in the three different densities.

To develop a scale for rating, you must have a good handle on the diversity you will encounter in the field. So make a preliminary survey and set down parameters for each number on the scale. Each class should encompass approximately an equal range of conditions.

Although rating is at times a somewhat subjective method of measuring, experimental error can be minimized by having the same observer rate an entire replication, adhering strictly to the parameters set forth in the rating scale. Numbers given by rating can be analyzed statistically in the same way as the numbers from any other type of measurement.

When rating, it is most effective to compare three different treatments. With two different treatments you do not get a good enough sense of the range of possibilities, while with more than three treatments the differences between plots tend to become fuzzy in your mind.

COLLECTING AND RECORDING DATA

Step eight is to collect and record data. A well-designed collection sheet, such as the one illustrated in Figure 9-7 for the pepper-density experiment, is a big help.

Randomized Data Collection

In the same way and for much the same reasons that you randomly place treatments in plots and randomly choose sampling units, you should also randomize the order in which you collect data. Though timing is probably not a critical factor when collecting ripe peppers, it becomes quite important when counting the number of slugs active in a garden or the number of insect pests on a plant.

The time of day and the type of weather account for different behavior patterns in soil animals. Your results, therefore, would likely be biased if you routinely observed your plots in the same order, visiting one at a certain time of day and the next a bit later.

With some kinds of observations and data collection you become more competent with practice, while with other tasks the routine leads to boredom and fatigue. In either case, the observations will not be made with equal efficiency. Balancing out this source of experimental error is another reason for alternating the order of data collection.

Precision in Data Collection

As you record data you may well wonder how exact you

Sample Data Collection Sheet for the Pepper Density Experiment

You will need 1 data sheet for each block of treatments (each replication).

		replication 1		
		treatments		
		(wts. of 4 sampling units recorded to nearest 1/4 lb.)		
dates of weekly observations	date of collection	A	B	C
	Aug. 15	1.50	1.75	0.50
	Aug. 22	3.75	4.50	0.75
	Aug. 29	2.50	4.75	1.25
	Sept. 5	3.50	5.25	3.75
	Sept. 12	4.25	6.75	4.00
	Sept. 19	6.75	8.00	3.75
	Sept. 26	3.00	4.25	3.25
	Oct. 3	1.75	2.75	1.50
The samples for each plot include 4 plants which are the sample units.	Oct. 10	0.75	0.00	0.50
	Oct. 17	4.25	2.00	5.75
	—frost Oct. 19	—	—	—
	total yield of sample	32.00	40.00	25.00
Divide the total yield by the number of plants (sample units).	mean yield plant	8.00	10.00	6.25
	total yield 6'x8' plot	x24 192.00	x18 180.00	x25 156.25

Multiply the mean yield by the number of plants in each plot.

weights recorded to nearest 1/4 lb.

Figure 9-7

need to be. Should you be talking in terms of pounds, pounds *and* ounces, or pounds *and* ounces *and* fractions of ounces? This is determined in part by the limitations of your tools. If you are measuring yields using a bathroom scale which is only dependably accurate to within a few pounds, then perhaps the weights should be recorded only to the nearest five pounds. Naturally this means you will have to deal with fairly large quantities at one time to compensate for the lack of detail. The heavier the sampling units, the less significant the pound or two which are rounded off. The more precise your measurements, the smaller the size of the sampling units that you will need.

A valuable rule of thumb is that the amount you round off should be less than one-fourth of the standard deviation, which is a measure of variability. Thus, once you have done some preliminary testing and have computed the standard deviation, you will have a guide for the rest of your data collection. For example, if the standard deviation is 13.6, one-fourth of that is 3.4 and the data need only be collected to the nearest whole unit. If the standard deviation is 1.3, one-fourth of that is 0.3 and the data should be recorded to the nearest one-tenth unit. The standard deviation and other statistics are calculated when you reach step nine.

ANALYZING RESULTS

Step nine is to analyze experimental results. The methods of statistical analysis which are presented here are both basic and quite simple to carry out. You will not need to make any complex calculations to determine the significance of your test results.

We sacrifice some precision in order to be able to use these simplified methods. This may result in your test results not being completely clear. If that is the case, or if you wish to do a more complete statistical analysis than is described here, see Cochran and Cox 1957, Cox 1958, Little and Hills 1975, Patterson 1939, or Snedecor and Cochran 1967.

Tabulating Data

Before beginning statistical analysis, you will have to tabulate your data by treatment. See Figures 9-8 through 9-11 for examples of data tables. Follow these steps to tabulate your data:

1. List the value of the data collected from each plot. The data can be a measure of yield, height, weight, number of individuals, or anything else that can be quantified.
2. Add the values for each treatment to find the treatment totals ($\Sigma\ x_i$).
3. Divide each treatment total by the number of ob-

(Continued on page 212)

Box 9-2: Some Symbols Used in Statistics

Greek letters are used to describe the "population," which is the entire group from which a sample is drawn. The letters of the English language alphabet are used to describe the sample.

"Statistics" is the branch of mathematics that uses probability theory as the basis for inferring truths about a population from sample data. When you calculate the mean, standard deviation, or other information from sample data, the value you arrive at is a "statistic." These statistics are used to estimate population parameters. A population parameter is defined by its mean and its standard deviation. These are definite values, but we seldom know what they are because most populations are too large to be completely measured. Instead we measure the mean and standard deviation of characteristics of the sample and use statistics to infer the values of the population mean and standard deviation.

x : an individual observation. When it has a subscript, e.g., x_3, the subscript designates which observation; in this case, the third observation of x.

x_i : all of the observations taken at one time; all of the variates.

$\bar{x}$: arithmetic mean of the sample. A straight line over any symbol indicates the mean or average.

r : range. The difference between the largest and smallest observations.

n : the total number of variates or sources of data. In field experiments this usually means the number of replications.

s, SD : standard deviation of the sample.

s^2 : variance of the sample. This is the square of the standard deviation.

$s_{\bar{x}}$, SE : standard error of the mean.

σ : (lower case of the Greek letter "sigma") standard deviation of the population.

(Continued)

σ^2	: variance of the population.
μ	: (lower case of the Greek letter "mu") mean of the population.
Σ	: (upper case of the Greek letter "sigma") sum, add together all of the values, e.g., "Σx_i" means add the values from all of the observations.

---

servations (n) to find the mean value for each treatment ($\bar{x}$).

4. Find the range of values for each treatment (r), which is the difference between the largest and smallest values.

5. Find the mean range ($\bar{r}$) by averaging the values for the treatment ranges.

6. When the standard deviation is calculated using the sum of squares method, you will need to square the value of each observation. This tabulation and method of calculating standard deviation are illustrated in Figure 9-9.

Calculating the Standard Deviation

A quick and easy method for calculating standard deviation is shown below. All you need to know is the mean range of your data, the number of replicates in your experiment, and the appropriate "range/standard deviation ratio" which you can get from the Table of Mean Values in Box 9-3. All that is required of you is one step of simple division.

The standard deviation that is calculated in this way is not as precise an estimate of the population standard deviation as is the standard deviation which is calculated by finding the sum of squares. This method is much, much easier to use, however, and the difference in precision can be made up by increasing the number of replications.

To compute an estimated standard deviation, follow these steps:

1. Tabulate your data by treatment.
2. Find the range of values for each treatment.
3. Find the mean range of all the treatments.
4. Find the appropriate "r/σ ratio" in Box 9-3.
5. Divide the mean range by the ratio given. This is the estimated standard deviation.

For example, Figure 9-8 is a tabulation of data given in Chapter 7 where we were counting the number of slugs in a garden with hiding places and comparing it with the number in a garden in the middle of an open field. Each of the circled numbers in the illustration refers to one of the steps listed above.

An Example of Computing Standard Deviation

treatments	total number of slugs trapped replications			(Σx_i) treatment totals	$(\bar{X})$ treatment means	(r) treatment range
	1	2	3			
garden with hiding places	108	99	88	295	98⅓	20
garden in open field	14	32	16	62	20⅔	18

mean $(\bar{r})$ range 19

④ 1.69 is the "r/σ ratio" where n = 3

⑤ standard deviation (SD) = mean range ÷ ratio of range : σ
  = 19 ÷ 1.69
  = 11.24

Figure 9-8

Testing for Significant Difference Between Treatments

The value you get for the standard deviation can be used in a simple test for significant difference between treatments. To decide if your treatments are significantly different, follow these steps:

1. Compute the standard deviation.

2. Find the "Standard Error of the Mean" (SE) by dividing the standard deviation (SD) by the square root of the number of samples (n). (The Table of Square Roots in Box 9-4 gives the square roots for numbers from 2 to 100.)

$$SE = SD/\sqrt{n}$$

3. Multiply the Standard Error of the Mean by 3.

4. If the difference between any two means is greater than three times the standard error, we can assume that there is a significant difference between the means and, therefore, between the treatment populations. (This test is taken from Jeffers 1960.)

For example: let us look again at the data on slugs caught in two different types of gardens.

1. The standard deviation was computed to be 11.24.

2. The standard error of the mean is:

$$SE = SD/\sqrt{n}$$
$$= 11.24/\sqrt{3}$$
$$= 6.49$$

3. $3 \times SE = 3 \times 6.49$
   $$= 19.47$$

4. The difference between the mean number of slugs caught in each type of garden is 77⅔ (98⅓ − 20⅔) = 77⅔. This is more than 19.47, so we can assume that the means are not estimates of the same population and that a significantly different number of slugs live in the two types of gardens.

Box 9-3: Table of Mean Values

Select a value from the right column to correspond with the number of samples (n) which you have collected. This value is used in the formula to compute standard deviation using the range/standard deviation ratio.

n	Mean Value of r/σ
2	1.13
3	1.69
4	2.06
5	2.33
6	2.53
7	2.70
8	2.85
9	2.97
10	3.08
15	3.47
20	3.73
30	4.09
50	4.50
75	4.81
100	5.02
150	5.3
200	5.5
300	5.8
500	6.1
700	6.3

Source: Snedecor and Cochran 1967 (cited in Jeffers 1960).

Using the Standard Deviation to Find Out Other Information about the Experimental Population

You can use the value computed for the standard deviation to predict the range of values which can be expected from a population. Let us use for an example a population of amaranth which is being sampled for yield data from 15 experimental plots in an area (see Figure 9-9). By calculating the mean yield and standard deviation from these 15

(Continued on page 222)

Box 9-4: Table of Square Roots

To compute the standard error of the mean, you need to know the square root of the number of samples in your experiment. Here is a list of the square roots of "n" for sample sizes from 2 to 100.

n	$\sqrt{n}$	n	$\sqrt{n}$	n	$\sqrt{n}$
2	1.414	35	5.916	68	8.246
3	1.732	36	6.000	69	8.307
4	2.000	37	6.083	70	8.367
5	2.236	38	6.164	71	8.426
6	2.449	39	6.245	72	8.485
7	2.646	40	6.325	73	8.544
8	2.828	41	6.403	74	8.602
9	3.000	42	6.481	75	8.660
10	3.162	43	6.557	76	8.718
11	3.317	44	6.633	77	8.775
12	3.464	45	6.708	78	8.832
13	3.606	46	6.782	79	8.888
14	3.742	47	6.856	80	8.944
15	3.873	48	6.928	81	9.000
16	4.000	49	7.000	82	9.055
17	4.123	50	7.071	83	9.110
18	4.243	51	7.141	84	9.165
19	4.359	52	7.211	85	9.220
20	4.472	53	7.280	86	9.274
21	4.583	54	7.348	87	9.327
22	4.690	55	7.416	88	9.381
23	4.796	56	7.483	89	9.434
24	4.899	57	7.550	90	9.487
25	5.000	58	7.616	91	9.539
26	5.099	59	7.681	92	9.592
27	5.196	60	7.746	93	9.644
28	5.292	61	7.810	94	9.695
29	5.385	62	7.874	95	9.747
30	5.477	63	7.937	96	9.798
31	5.568	64	8.000	97	9.849
32	5.657	65	8.062	98	9.899
33	5.745	66	8.124	99	9.950
34	5.831	67	8.185	100	10.000

Two Methods of Computing Standard Deviation

Tabulation of data from 15 plots of amaranth: Each plot is 1/1000 acre and contains 32 plants. Yield from all the plants is measured at the end of the season.

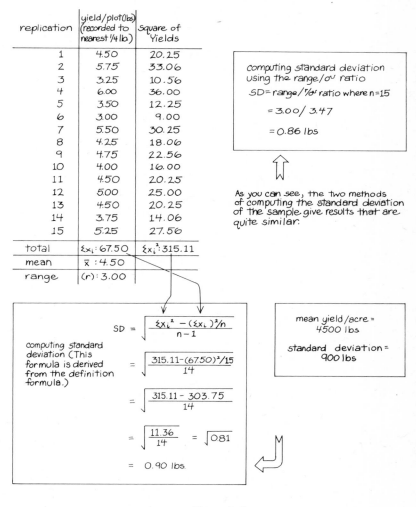

replication	yield/plot(lbs) (recorded to nearest 1/4 lb.)	Square of Yields
1	4.50	20.25
2	5.75	33.06
3	3.25	10.56
4	6.00	36.00
5	3.50	12.25
6	3.00	9.00
7	5.50	30.25
8	4.25	18.06
9	4.75	22.56
10	4.00	16.00
11	4.50	20.25
12	5.00	25.00
13	4.50	20.25
14	3.75	14.06
15	5.25	27.56
total	Σx_i: 67.50	Σx_i^2: 315.11
mean	$\bar{x}$: 4.50	
range	(r): 3.00	

computing standard deviation using the range/σ ratio

SD = range/r/σ ratio where n=15

$$= 3.00 / 3.47$$

$$= 0.86 \text{ lbs}$$

As you can see, the two methods of computing the standard deviation of the sample give results that are quite similar.

computing standard deviation (This formula is derived from the definition formula.)

$$SD = \sqrt{\frac{\Sigma x_i^2 - (\Sigma x_i)^2/n}{n-1}}$$

$$= \sqrt{\frac{315.11 - (67.50)^2/15}{14}}$$

$$= \sqrt{\frac{315.11 - 303.75}{14}}$$

$$= \sqrt{\frac{11.36}{14}} = \sqrt{0.81}$$

$$= 0.90 \text{ lbs}$$

mean yield/acre = 4500 lbs

standard deviation = 900 lbs

Figure 9-9

Box 9-5: Tabulation of the Data and Analysis of the Pepper-Density Experiment

1. Table of the Mean Yield per Pepper Plant (measured to nearest ¼ pound)
2. Calculations
   a. Estimated standard deviation using the "range/standard deviation ratio (r/σ)":

$$SD = \frac{\text{mean range}}{\text{mean value of r/}\sigma}$$
where n = 4

$$= 1.50/2.06$$

$$= 0.73 \text{ pounds}$$

   b. Standard error of the mean:
$$SE = SD/\sqrt{n}$$
$$= 0.73/\sqrt{4}$$
$$= 0.36 \text{ pounds}$$

   c. Simple test for significant difference: if 3(SE)<the difference between two treatment means, the treatments are significantly different.

Table of Mean Yield for the Pepper Density Experiment

treatments	mean yield / plant–season total (weight in lbs.)				treatment totals (Σx_i)	treatment means ($\bar{x}$)	treatment range (r)
	replications						
	1	2	3	4			
A	8.00	7.75	8.50	8.75	33.00	8.5	1.00
B	10.00	9.25	8.75	10.75	38.75	9.7	2.00
C	6.25	5.50	5.25	6.75	23.75	5.9	1.50
block totals:	24.25	22.50	22.50	26.25	grand total: 95.50		mean range: 1.50

Figure 9-10

3(SE) = 3(0.36) = 1.08 = 1.1 pounds

The difference between the means of Treatments A and B is 1.2 pounds; between A and C, 2.6 pounds; and between B and C, 3.8 pounds. Therefore we can conclude that all the treatments are significantly different.

3. Conclusions

a. Each of the treatments is significantly different.

b. Treatment B, with the lowest planting density, has the highest yield per plant.

c. Planting closer together than the recommended density tends to decrease the yield per plant.

d. The significant difference between Treatments A and C seems to indicate that the arrangement of plants within the plot is important in determining yield since both of these treatments had virtually the same planting density.

4. Table of Yield per Plot (measured to nearest ¼ pound)

Yield per plot is computed by multiplying the mean yield per plant by the number of plants in the plot.

5. Calculations

a. Estimated standard deviation using the "range/standard deviation ratio (r/σ)":

$$SD = \frac{\text{mean range}}{\text{mean value of } r/\sigma}$$
where n = 4

= 32.50/2.06

= 15.78 pounds

b. Standard error of the mean:

$$SE = SD/\sqrt{n}$$
= 15.78/$\sqrt{4}$

= 7.89 pounds

(Continued)

Table of Yield Per Plot for the Pepper Density Experiment

Treatments	yield / plot - season total (weight in lbs.)				treatment totals (ξX_i)	treatment means $(\bar{X})$	treatment range (r)
	replications						
	1	2	3	4			
A 24 plants/ plot	192.00	186.00	204.00	210.00	792.00	198.0	24.00
B 18 plants/ plot	180.00	166.50	157.50	193.50	697.50	174.0	36.00
C 25 plants/ plot	156.25	137.50	131.25	168.75	593.75	148.4	37.50
block totals:	528.25	490.00	492.75	572.25	grand total: 2,083.25		mean range: 32.50

Figure 9-11

c. Simple test for significant difference: if the difference between two treatment means > 3(SE), that indicates a significant difference between the two treatments.

$$3(SE) = 3(7.89) = 23.67 \text{ pounds}$$

The difference between the means of Treatments B and C is 25.6 pounds and between Treatments A and C is 49.6 pounds. Both Treatments A and B are significantly different from Treatment C.

The difference between the means of Treatments A and B is 24.00 pounds. It is too close to 23.67 pounds to be able to conclude with certainty that there is a significant difference between Treatments A and B. The data will have to go through an "analysis of variance" which is a much more precise statistical analysis. It is explained in most statistics textbooks.

6. Calculating Cost Efficiency

Even if we assume that there is a significant difference between Treatments A and B (since the "range/standard deviation ratio" often overestimates standard deviation), we cannot recommend planting in the arrangement of Treatment A until we make certain it is cost effective.

If I paid $.10 per pepper plant and used six more plants in plots with Treatment A than in plots with Treatment B, I must get at least $.60 more worth of peppers from the "A" plots in order to make that planting arrangement worthwhile.

If there were any other expenses particular to one of the treatments, I would have to include their costs in these calculations as well.

If peppers are worth $.20/pound, then I would need only an average of 3 extra pounds on the average from Treatment A to pay for the extra cost of seedlings. As it is, with an average of 24 more pounds of peppers from Treatment A, the additional produce is worth $4.80.

Finally, before recommending this planting arrangement I must take into consideration any problems it might have that would detract from the attractive feature of increased yield: are there any problems with cultivating, harvesting, or disease?

7. Calculation of Percentage Improvement

To calculate the percent improvement in yield of Treatment A over Treatment B, divide the mean difference between the yields by the yield of Treatment B:

$$\frac{\text{mean difference}}{\text{lower yield}} = \frac{24}{174} = 14 \text{ percent}$$

8. Conclusion

It can be predicted that on the average peppers planted in the arrangement of Treatment A will

(Continued)

have a 14 percent higher yield than peppers planted in the density traditionally recommended, and that this increased yield makes Treatment A cost effective.

(The data used in this example are hypothetical, so do not change your habits with regard to pepper-planting based on the results of this experiment.)

plots, we can make predictions about the yield of amaranth in our region. To make these predictions more applicable, let's convert yield per 1/1,000 acre plot to yield per acre by multiplying by 1,000. The yield per acre is computed to be 4,500 pounds with a standard deviation of 900 pounds. Assuming that this sample data accurately reflect the yield of amaranth in this population, we can now predict:

- In more than two-thirds of all cases, the amaranth yield will be between 3,600 and 5,400 pounds per acre. This is the range of values found by subtracting 1 standard deviation from the mean yield (4,500 pounds minus 900 pounds equals 3,600 pounds) and by adding 1 standard deviation to the mean yield (4,500 pounds plus 900 pounds equals 5,400 pounds). In a normal population about two-thirds of all cases fall within this range of the mean ±1 standard deviation.
- In more than 80 percent of all cases, the yield will be greater than 3,600 pounds per acre. This is computed as the mean minus 1 standard deviation.
- The minimum yield that can be expected from an acre of amaranth is 1,800 pounds. This is computed by multiplying the standard deviation by 3 and subtracting the result from the mean. In only three cases out of 1,000 will the yield be less than this.

You can use these same calculations to make predictions about other normally distributed populations once you have a good estimate of the mean and standard deviation.

(Continued on page 225)

Box 9-6: 95 Percent Confidence Intervals for the True Proportion of Success

This table is used when your data give just a "yes" or a "no" answer rather than a numerical value. For example, say you have 100 beehives. It is March and you want to know how many of your colonies survived the winter. It is a big job to open up and check 100 hives, so you randomly choose 30 of the hives to examine. You might find that 80 percent or 24 colonies of bees are still alive, but it would be presumptuous of you to therefore conclude that 80 of your 100 hives have survived. With a different sample of 30 hives, you would perhaps have found a few more or less than 24 of the colonies still living.

Although there is no way you can predict the exact number of surviving hives without sampling them all, you can have confidence in the range of successes given on this table.

Observed No. of Successes	For 30 Trials True Proportion of Success Is Between	For 50 Trials True Proportion of Success Is Between
0	0.00 and 0.12	0.00 and 0.07
1	0.00 and 0.17	0.00 and 0.11
2	0.01 and 0.22	0.00 and 0.14
3	0.02 and 0.27	0.01 and 0.17
4	0.04 and 0.31	0.02 and 0.19
5	0.06 and 0.35	0.03 and 0.22
6	0.08 and 0.39	0.05 and 0.24
7	0.10 and 0.42	0.06 and 0.27
8	0.12 and 0.46	0.07 and 0.29
9	0.15 and 0.49	0.09 and 0.31
10	0.17 and 0.53	0.10 and 0.34
11	0.20 and 0.56	0.12 and 0.36
12	0.23 and 0.59	0.13 and 0.38
13	0.25 and 0.63	0.15 and 0.40
14	0.28 and 0.66	0.16 and 0.42
15	0.31 and 0.69	0.18 and 0.45
16	0.34 and 0.72	0.19 and 0.47

(Continued)

Observed No. of Successes	For 30 Trials True Proportion of Success Is Between	For 50 Trials True Proportion of Success Is Between
17	0.37 and 0.75	0.21 and 0.49
18	0.41 and 0.77	0.23 and 0.51
19	0.43 and 0.80	0.25 and 0.53
20	0.47 and 0.83	0.26 and 0.55
21	0.51 and 0.85	0.28 and 0.57
22	0.54 and 0.88	0.30 and 0.59
23	0.58 and 0.90	0.32 and 0.61
24	0.61 and 0.92	0.34 and 0.63
25	0.65 and 0.94	0.36 and 0.64
26	0.69 and 0.96	0.37 and 0.66
27	0.73 and 0.98	0.39 and 0.68
28	0.78 and 0.99	0.41 and 0.70
29	0.83 and 1.00	0.43 and 0.72
30	0.88 and 1.00	0.45 and 0.74
31		0.47 and 0.75
32		0.49 and 0.77
33		0.51 and 0.79
34		0.53 and 0.80
35		0.55 and 0.82
36		0.58 and 0.84
37		0.60 and 0.85
38		0.62 and 0.87
39		0.64 and 0.88
40		0.66 and 0.90
41		0.69 and 0.91
42		0.71 and 0.93
43		0.73 and 0.94
44		0.76 and 0.95
45		0.78 and 0.97
46		0.81 and 0.98
47		0.83 and 0.99
48		0.86 and 1.00
49		0.89 and 1.00
50		0.93 and 1.00

Source: Creech 1974.

Based on your having looked at 30 hives (trials) and having found 24 living (successes), it is highly likely that between 61 and 92 of your hives are actually thriving. We find this information by locating "24" in the first column and looking across to the second column where it says "0.61 and 0.92."

If you had examined a larger number of hives, say 50, the confidence interval would be narrower. In this case, if 40 of the 50 hives were alive, you would be pretty safe in assuming that a total of between 66 and 90 of your colonies were living. With a finite number of beehives, you actually could examine them all if you wanted to and count the actual number of living hives.

You do not have this option in all cases. With seed germination experiments, for example, you obviously cannot test all of your seeds. If you did, you would not have any seed left to grow your plants. In cases like this you must depend on the information given by the confidence intervals.

With some effort, confidence intervals can be calculated for samples of any size, but in order to use this table you must have either 30 or 50 variates, each one of which says either "yes" or "no," "success" or "failure."

WRITING YOUR REPORT

Step ten is to write a report. This is the final step in research work. It need not be elaborate, but it should contain information about how the experiment was conducted, the results of any statistical analysis, and a critique of the procedures used. You may be surprised at how writing down this information helps to clarify your thoughts about what was accomplished.

The report complements your research notebook or working file which contains all the raw data and calculations as well as field observations.

By following a somewhat standard format, your report will be more intelligible to others who might want to read it or to a statistician who might be doing further analysis of your data. A possible format is:

Title

Purpose of the Experiment:

goals

hypotheses tested

treatments compared

Literature Review:

published or unpublished sources on which you may have based ideas or assumptions.

Methods:

experimental design—type, number of replications, how and where it was laid out

details on materials or procedures used

variables assessed

number of sample units and how they were chosen

charts of data

Results:

tabulations of data

graphs

statistical tests

nontabulated observations

Discussion:

critique all the above points; in other words, discuss whether the design was suitable, whether you collected the right data at the right time, what you should have done differently, and what worked well. Discuss the results.

Conclusion:

the conclusion should contain only concise statements which can be drawn from the data of your experiment.

If you are considering writing up your research report for publication in a scientific journal, consult a style manual such as that prepared by the Council of Biology Editors (1972).

Appendix I: Supplies

Sometimes, in the course of your experimentation, you might want a piece of equipment that is not available in your local hardware or gardening supply outlet. If you cannot make an adequate substitute (or find something in your kitchen or garage to use instead), it is helpful to know about the suppliers of different types of goods and gadgetry.

The following annotated list of suppliers of biological and scientific equipment covers a wide variety of companies. Some are geared for the individual and hobbyist, others primarily for schools, laboratories, or industry. While all of these companies deal with individual purchasers, some require a minimum order. Some of the suppliers do not sell chemicals to individuals except in small quantities already packaged into kits. You will probably be able to find some of these catalogs in the science department of your local public school or college.

Brookstone Company
127 Vose Farm Rd.
Peterborough, NH 03458   (603) 924-7181

Their catalog of "hard-to-find tools and other fine things" is geared to the hobbyist and craftsperson. Included with its vast array of gadgetry from all fields are some gardening tools, weather monitoring equipment, magnifier loupes, and microprobe sets for dissection of plants and animals.

Carolina Biological Supply Company
Burlington, NC 27216   (919) 584-0381

or

Carolina Biological Supply Company
c/o Powell Labs.
Gladstone, OR 97027   (503) 656-1641

Their products are designed primarily for university and laboratory audiences. The products of interest to us are the plant and insect collecting and preserving equipment, soil-testing kits, an array of equipment for monitoring the weather, as well as all types of laboratory glassware and chemicals. Orders from individuals are taken for a minimum of $15 plus 20 percent handling. Chemicals by themselves are not sold to individuals. (You could not, for example, buy the chemicals to make your own insect-killing jars, but you could buy the killing jars already prepared.)

DuMaurier Company
P. O. Box 4010
Virginia Beach, VA 23454   (804) 422-6533

Manufacturers of "pen microscopes" from 10x to 50x, made with or without measuring scales. Great little tools!

Edmund Scientific Company
7897 Edscorp Building
Barrington, NJ 08007   (609) 547-3488

Their claim is to "over 4,000 unique products for hobbyists, schools, and industry" including a soil-testing kit, laboratory glassware, dissecting kits, weather monitoring equipment, a great variety of optical equipment, magnets, and a tremendous variety in their field of specialty, astronomy.

Fisher Scientific Company
15 Jet View Dr.
Rochester, NY 14624   (716) 464-8900

This company has branch offices all over the country. Their offerings in the biological field are similar to those of the Carolina Biological Supply Company.

Forestry Suppliers
Box 8397
Jackson, MS 39204   (601) 354-3565

Theirs wares are meant for the forester. Among other items, they carry knives, compasses, surveying equipment, altimeters, barometers, wind and water meters, and soil-testing equipment.

Horizon Ecology Company
7435 N. Oak Park Ave.
Chicago, IL 60648   (312) 647-7644

They sell meters and kits for analyzing chemicals and metals in water, soil, and air and also deal with laboratory equipment. They offer fairly sophisticated laboratory machinery which appears to be aimed to an industry and government clientele.

Insect Museum Supply
Jack R. Powers
1021 8th Ave.
South Moorhead, MN 56560   (218) 236-6620

Specialty supplier of custom-printed insect pin labels, microscope slide labels, and insect pins.

Scientific Products
Division of American Hospital Supply Corporation
1430 Waukegan Rd.
McGraw Park, IL 60085   (312) 689-8410

For our interests they have magnifiers, weather monitoring equipment, and chemicals, as well as a tremendous stock of laboratory supplies.

Turtox/Cambosco
MacMillan Science Company, Inc.
8200 S. Hoyne Ave.
Chicago, IL 60620   toll-free number: (800) 621-8980

This company is oriented to the sale of teaching supplies for biology classes on the high school and college level, and offers a complete selection of insect collecting equipment and magnifiers. They do not sell chemicals to individuals.

The Urbana Laboratories
Box 299, Triumph Dr.
Urbana, IL 61801   (217) 367-3046, or 367-3032

They sell the "NPK Plant Test Kit for detecting nutrient starvation in plants using the color-strip plant leaf analysis method." They also sell chemicals and equipment for soil testing.

Wards' Natural Science Establishment, Inc.
P. O. Box 1712
Rochester, NY 14603   (716) 467-8400

        or

Wards' of California
P. O. Box 1749
Monterey, CA 93942   (408) 375-7294

Their selection is similar to that of Carolina Biological Supply Company.

Appendix II: Organizations

This is a list of groups which in some way or another are involved with or supportive of participatory research.

Agway Seed Department
P. O. Box 4933
Syracuse, NY 13221

Agway maintains an extensive research and development program both on its own farms and through the efforts of cooperating food growers in the 12-state Northeast region. Fred Williams, supervisor of the vegetable seed research program, is always on the lookout for "cooperators" who would be willing to grow test varieties on their land and record the data requested.

Other seed companies in your area may also have "cooperator" programs.

American Horticultural Society
Mt. Vernon, VA 22121

This society publishes the *Directory of American Horticulture* which lists national organizations with interests in specific types of plants, such as the African Violet Society of America, the American Rose Society, the Northern Nut Growers Association, etc. If you want to become involved with breeding and cultural experiments on a specific type of plant, this is a great way to get in touch with people of like mind. Regional chapters of these groups are often represented at county and state fairs.

Henry Doubleday Research Association
20 Covent Ln.
Bocking, Braintree
Essex, England

Founded in 1954, this group now has some 6,500 members (including three groups in Australia and one each in India and New Zealand). It is involved with participatory research projects on subjects such as: the utilization of Russian comfrey, comparing methods of soil cultivation, companion planting, an indexing of all the fruit and vegetable varieties available in Britain, comparing methods of growing potatoes, and amassing information on tree farming in different climatic zones. The primary objective is the improvement of organic techniques of agriculture and horticulture. Membership is $10/year.

International Federation of Organic Agricultural Movements
(IFOAM)
P. O. Box 124
Hallowell, ME 04347

This is "an organization of groups and individuals from around the world, united in their goal to seek an alternative to the current forms of agriculture." The brief articles in their fascinating quarterly newsletter ($7/year) often report on just the type of research work of interest to the ambitious backyard gardener and small-scale farmer. This newsletter is an invaluable resource for the inquisitive organic agriculturalist who seeks contact with others involved in researching.

North American Fruit Explorers (NAFEX)
10 S. 55 Madison St.
Hinsdale, IL 60521

This is an organization of people interested in growing fruit and nut trees. Members collect and propagate fruit and nut trees which they have found on abandoned homesteads and work towards developing seedlings that are resistant to disease and insect damage. Membership fees and a subscription to their newsletter are $5/year.

Northern Nut Growers Association
4518 Holston Hills Rd.
Knoxville, TN 37914

Also an organization of nut tree enthusiasts, some of their members are involved with the efforts to select for a resistant American chestnut tree.

Rodale Reader Research Projects
Research and Development
33 E. Minor St.
Emmaus, PA 18049

Working in conjunction with researchers at the Organic Gardening and Farming Research Center, the reader research projects have involved thousands of people to date, most of them on a project to test the adaptability of amaranth to a wide variety of growing conditions. Since 1975, backyard researchers have been looking into different questions regarding the cultivation of amaranth. Other reader research projects have included testing for resistant varieties, working out the correct spacing and density of companion plants, and developing backyard fisheries.

Seed Savers Exchange
c/o Kent Whealy
RFD 2 (HS)
Princeton, MO 64673

Previously known as the True Seed Exchange, this is "an organization of vegetable gardeners who are dedicated to finding, multiplying, and spreading 'heirloom' vegetable varieties before they are lost forever." Kent Whealy publishes an annual yearbook with the names of members and the vegetable varieties they have available for exchange with other members. The yearbook also contains a "hodge-podge" section with news of the work of many backyard researchers. You can be a member only if you have seed to offer, but nonmembers can subscribe to the yearbook for $2 and can also buy seeds from the members for a small fee. The hope is that nonmembers will begin to save the heirloom seeds and make them available to others so that they too can become members. The types of seeds the group is looking for are: vegetable varieties that have been handed down in a family over a long period of time; varieties that are no longer available in seed catalogs; varieties that people have improved upon over the years; very resistant or hardy varieties; and varieties from other parts of the world.

Soil and Health Foundation
33 E. Minor St.
Emmaus, PA 18049

This is a small, nonprofit organization which solicits contributions to give as grants to researchers working on projects of benefit to organic agriculture. Thus far grants have only gone to researchers in an academic setting, but that is not a criterion for application.

Wannigan Associates
c/o John Withee
262 Salem St.
Lynnfield, MA 01940

This group collects, propagates and distributes the seeds of heirloom beans. For $5 a year members get the annual catalog, a quarterly newsletter, two heirloom bean varieties of their choice and two other varieties to grow for seed renewal. The seeds from these renewal plants are to be returned to the organization after which the grower can request another two varieties.

Bibliography

Agricultural and horticultural seeds. 1961. FAO Agricultural Studies no. 55. Rome, Italy.

Allard, R. W. 1960. *Principles of plant breeding.* New York: John Wiley & Sons.

Alverson, D. R.; All, J. N.; and Mathews, R. W. 1977. *Journal of the Georgia entomological society* 12:336–341.

American men and women of science. 1976. 13th ed. 7 vols. Edited by Jaques Cattell Press. New York: R. R. Bowker Co.

Austin, R. B.; Longden, P. C.; and Hutchinson, J. 1969. Some effects of "hardening" carrot seed. *Annals of botany* 33:883–95.

Baker, W. L. 1972. *Eastern forest insects.* USDA Forest Service Miscellaneous Publication no. 1175.
  Excellent publication identifying and giving biological information on specific tree pests.

Bandel, V. A. et al. 1975. N behavior under no-till vs. conventional corn culture. I. First-year results using unlabeled N fertilizer. *Agronomy journal* 67:782–86.

Barnes, H. F., and Weil, J. W. 1942. Baiting slugs using metal-dehyde mixed with various substances. *Annals of applied biology* 29:56–68.

———. 1944. Slugs in gardens: their numbers, activities and distribution. Part I. *Journal of animal ecology* 13:140–75.

Good natural history information with descriptions and a key to the common slugs of the British Isles; also describes collection techniques.

———. 1945. Slugs in gardens: their numbers, activities and distribution. Part II. *Journal of animal ecology* 14:71–105.

More discussion of natural history of slugs, especially their feeding and mating habits.

Barnothy, M. F., ed. 1964. *Biological effects of magnetic fields.* 2 vols. New York: Plenum Publications.

Berrie, A. M. M., and Drenna, D. S. H. 1971. The effect of hydration-dehydration on seed germination. *New phytologist* 70:135–42.

Blackwelder, R. E., and Blackwelder, R. M., eds. 1961. *Directory of zoological taxonomists of the world.* Carbondale, Illinois: Southern Illinois Univ. Press.

Blanchard, J. R., and Ostvold, H. 1958. *Literature of agricultural research.* Berkeley: Univ. of California Press.

Bonn, G. S., ed. 1973. *Information resources in the environmental sciences.* Allerton Park Institute no. 18. Champaign, Illinois: Univ. of Illinois Graduate School of Library Science.

Borror, D. J.; Delong, D. M.; and Triplehorn, C. A. 1976. *An introduction to the study of insects.* 4th ed. New York: Holt, Rinehart & Winston.

Identification keys, biological information, and technical aids for working with insects and other arthropods. Insects are keyed to family; other arthropods to order.

Borror, D. J., and White, R. E. 1970. *A field guide to the insects of America north of Mexico.* Peterson Field Guide Series. Boston: Houghton Mifflin Co.

Excellent field guide with picture keys.

Bottle, R. T. 1972. *The use of biological literature.* 2d ed. Woburn, Massachusetts: Butterworths Publishing.

Brady, N. C. 1974. *The nature and properties of soils*. 8th ed. New York: Macmillan Publishing Co.

Breeding plants for home and garden: a handbook. 1974. *Plants and gardens* 30:1. Brooklyn, New York: Brooklyn Botanic Garden.

Bromfield, L. 1976. (reprint of 1945 ed.) *Pleasant valley*. Mattituck, New York: Amereon.

Bubel, N. 1978. *The seed-starter's handbook*. Emmaus, Pennsylvania: Rodale Press.

Burch, J. B. 1962. *How to know the eastern land snails*. Picture-Key Nature Series. Dubuque, Iowa: William C. Brown Co.

The most accessible reference on slugs outside the academic world. Presents some general natural history and biological information along with a good, easy-to-use illustrated key to slug and snail identification in the United States east of the Rocky Mountain Divide.

Buxton, D. R. et al. 1977. Evaluation of seed treatments to enhance Pima cotton seedling emergence. *Agronomy journal* 69:672–76.

Causey, D. 1961. The earthworms of Arkansas. Pp. 43–56 *in* R. Rodale, ed., *The challenge of earthworm research*. Emmaus, Pennsylvania: The Soil and Health Foundation.

Contains identification key.

Chemical abstracts service source index. 1975. Columbus, Ohio: Chemical Abstracts Service, Division of the American Chemical Society.

Chiang, H. C. 1977. *Pest management in the People's Republic of China: monitoring and forecasting insect populations in rice, wheat, cotton and maize*. FAO Plant Protection Bulletin 25:1–8.

Information translated from a Chinese publication on integrated control methods useful for 22 major insect pests.

Chippingdale, H. G. 1933. The effect of soaking in water on the "seeds" of *Dactylis glomerata*. *Annals of botany* 47:841–49.

———. 1934. The effect of soaking in water on the "seeds" of some Gramineae. *Annals of applied biology* 21:225–32.

Clausen, C. P. 1956. *Biological control of insect pests in the continental United States.* Washington, D.C.: USDA Agricultural Technical Bulletin no. 1139.

Cochran, W. G., and Cox, G. M. 1957. *Experimental designs.* 2d ed. New York: John Wiley & Sons.

Council of Biology Editors Committee on Form & Style. 1972. *CBE style manual.* 3d ed. Washington, D.C.: American Institute of Biological Sciences.

Cox, D. R. 1958. *Planning of experiments.* New York: John Wiley & Sons.

Creech, F. R. 1974. Backyard organic research. *Organic gardening and farming.* 21:126–30.

Crookston, K. 1977. Ancient practice of intercropping makes comeback. *IFOAM Bulletin 20.*

Cumulative book index: a world list of books in the English language. Annual. New York: H. W. Wilson Co.

Davidson, R. H., and Peairs, L. M. 1966. *Insect pests of farm, garden, & orchard.* 6th ed. New York: John Wiley & Sons.
Biological characteristics and identification by species.

DeBach, P., and Schlinger, E. I., eds. 1964. *Biological control of insect pests and weeds.* New York: Reinhold Publishing Co.

Eddy, S., and Hodson, A. C. 1961. *Taxonomic keys to the common animals of the north central states.* Minneapolis, Minnesota: Burgess Publishing Co.

Edwards, C. A., and Lofty, J. R. 1972. *Biology of earthworms.* London: Chapman & Hall.
Pages 212–18 contain a simplified key to common earthworms.

Eggert, F. P. 1977. The effect of several soil management systems on soil parameters and on the productivity of crops. *IFOAM Bulletins* 20 and 22.

Falk, J. H. 1976. Energetics of a suburban lawn ecosystem. *Ecology* 57:141–50.
Production and energy input for a suburban lawn are assessed.

Faulkner, E. H. 1943. *Plowman's folly.* New York: Grosset & Dunlap.

Fisher, R. A., and Yates, F. 1974. *Statistical tables for biological, agricultural, & medical research.* 6th ed. New York: Hafner Publishing Co.

Fisher, T. W. 1960. "What is biological control?" Pp. 6–18 *in* C. Westcott, ed., *Handbook on biological control of plant pests.* Special printing of *Plants and gardens* 16:3. Brooklyn, New York: Brooklyn Botanic Garden.

Foth, H. D. 1978. *Fundamentals of soil science.* 6th ed. New York: John Wiley & Sons.

Galtsoff, P. S. et al. 1937. *Culture methods for invertebrate animals.* Ithaca, New York: Comstock Publishing Associates.
A compilation of papers, each one of which covers ways to rear a particular organism or group of organisms; designed for researchers, teachers, and zoos, but valuable to anyone who wants to mass-rear parasitoids or predators or food for fish in a fisheries project.

Gates, J. K. 1973. *Guide to the use of books and libraries.* 3d ed. McGraw-Hill Series in Library Science. New York: McGraw-Hill Book Co.

Geiger, R. 1965. *The climate near the ground.* Cambridge, Massachusetts: Harvard Univ. Press.

Genkel, P. A.; Martyanova, K. L.; and Zubova, L. S. 1964. Production experiments on presowing drought hardening of plants. *Fiziologiya rastenii (Soviet plant physiology)* 11:538.

Gray, D., and Steckel, J. R. A. 1977. Effects of presowing treatments of seeds on the germination and establishment of parsnips. *Journal of horticultural science* 52:525–34.

Grimm, W. C. 1968. *Recognizing flowering wild plants.* New York: Stackpole Books.

Grogan, D. 1973. *Science and technology: an introduction to the literature.* Hamden, Connecticut: Linnet Books.

Hayes, H. K., and Immer, F. R. 1942. *Methods of plant breeding.* New York: McGraw-Hill Book Co.

Heichel, G. H. 1973. *Comparative efficiency of energy use in crop production.* Connecticut Agricultural Extension Station Bulletin no. 739.
Caloric input-caloric output ratios compared in 15 agricultural

systems using data from previous studies. Excellent bibliography.

Hopp, H. 1954. *A guide to extensive testing on farms in 4 parts.* 3 vols. USDA Forest Agricultural Service.

Jaques, H. E. 1958. *How to know the economic plants.* Picture-Key Nature Series. Dubuque, Iowa: William C. Brown Co.

Javits, T. 1977. Green grass or alfalfa? A comparison study. *The Farallones Institute Report:* Pp. 21–22. (15290 Coleman Valley Road, Occidental, CA 95465).

Calculates a 16-fold energy return on a planting of alfalfa in the strip between the street and sidewalk in front of a house in Berkeley, California. Large return primarily due to use of human rather than machine labor.

Jeavons, J. 1979. *How to grow more vegetables than you ever thought posssible on less land than you can imagine.* Berkeley, California: Ten Speed Press.

Jeffers, J. N. R. 1960. *Experimental design and analysis in forest research.* Stockholm, Sweden: Almquist & Wiksell.

Johnson, W. A.; Stolzfus, V.; and Craymer, P. 1977. Energy conservation in Amish agriculture. *Science* 198:373–78.

Commercial farms of the Amish compared with those of their neighbors.

Johnston, R., Jr. 1976. *Growing garden seeds: A manual for gardeners and small farmers.* Albion, Maine: Johnny's Selected Seeds, Organic Seed and Crop Research.

Kaston, B. J. 1948. *Spiders of Connecticut.* Hartford, Connecticut: State Geological and Natural History Survey of Connecticut.

Excellent for identification and information on spiders; valuable far beyond the borders of Connecticut.

Kaston, B. J., and Kaston, E. 1978. *How to know the spiders.* 3d ed. Picture-Key Nature Series. Dubuque, Iowa: William C. Brown Co.

A complete, well-illustrated field and laboratory guide to spider identification.

Kiesselbach, T. A. 1923. Competition as a source of error in comparative corn tests. *Journal of the American Society of Agronomists* 15:199–215.

Krantz, B. A.; Nelson, W. L.; and Burkhart, L. 1948. Plant tissue tests as a tool in agronomy research. Pp. 137–56 *in* Bear, F. E. et al., *Diagnostic techniques for soils and crops.* Washington, D.C.: American Potash Institute.

Kring, J. B. 1970. Red spheres and yellow panels combined to attract apple maggot flies. *Journal of economic entomology* 63:466–69.

A good example of the logic used in developing a trap for a particular insect pest.

Lappé, F. M. 1975. *Diet for a small planet.* rev. ed. New York: Ballantine Books.

Lasworth, E. J. 1972. *Reference sources in science and technology.* Metuchen, New Jersey: Scarecrow Press.

Lebedev, S. I. et al. 1975. Physiobiochemical characteristics of plants after presowing treatment with a permanent magnetic field. *Soviet plant physiology* 22:84–89.

LeClerg, E. L.; Leonard, W. H.; and Clark, A. G. 1962. *Field plot technique.* 2d ed. Minneapolis, Minnesota: Burgess Publishing Co.

Levi, H. W. 1966. The care of alcohol collections of small invertebrates. *Systematic zoology* 15:183–88.

Good source of information on preservation techniques.

Library of Congress subject headings. 2 vols. 8th ed. 1975. Subject Cataloging Division—Processing Department. Washington, D.C.: Library of Congress.

Little, T. M., and Hills, F. J. 1975. *Statistical methods in agricultural research.* 2d ed. Davis, California: Univ. of California at Davis Bookstore.

Lockeretz, W., ed. 1977. *Agriculture and energy.* New York: Academic Press.

Compilation of many energy studies presented at a conference on agriculture and energy held at Washington University, St. Louis, Missouri, June 17–19, 1976.

Lovell, H. B. 1956. *Honey plants manual: a practical field handbook for identifying honey flora.* Medina, Ohio: A. I. Root Co.

Lovins, A. B. 1975. *World energy strategies: facts, issues, & options.* Energy Papers Series. Cambridge, Massachusetts: Ballinger Publishing Co. (copublished by Friends of the Earth)

A lively but serious consideration of present energy use and possible future sources.

Mercer, W. B., and Hall, A. D. 1911. Experimental error in field trials. *Journal of agricultural science* 4:107–27.

Metcalf, C. L.; Flint, W. P.; and Metcalf, R. L. 1962. *Destructive & useful insects: their habits and control.* 4th ed. New York: McGraw-Hill Book Co.

A useful book because of the biological information on specific pests. Unfortunately, advises chemical control.

Meyer, J. E. 1968. *The herbalist.* rev. ed. New York: Sterling Publishing Co.

Miller, D. C. 1977. *Vegetable and herb seed growing for the gardener and small farmer.* Hersey, Michigan: Bullkill Creek Publishing Co.

Miller, W. H.; Bernard, G. D.; and Allen, J. L. 1968. The optics of insect compound eyes. *Science* 162:76–77.

How insect vision works.

Moore, H. S., and Noblet, R. 1974. Flight range of *Simulium slossanae* the primary vector of *Leucocytozoon smithi* of turkeys in South Carolina. *Environmental entomology* 3:365–69.

Source of information on the "sticky traps" for flying insects which are discussed in Chapter 7.

Moorehouse, L. A., and Juve, O. A. 1921. *Labor and materials requirements of field crops.* USDA Bulletin no. 1000.

Morris, J. M., and Elkins, E. A. 1978. *Literature searching: resources & strategies with examples from the environmental sciences.* Library Resources Series. New York: Jeffrey Norton Publishing.

Naturalists' directory (international). 1975. 42d ed. Marlton, New Jersey: World Natural History Publications.

Newell, P. F. 1971. "Mollusks" Pp. 128–49 *in* J. Philipson, ed., *Methods of study in quantitative soil ecology: population, production and energy flow.* International Biological Program Handbook no. 18. Oxford, England: Blackwell Scientific Publications.

Research and field methods for assessing population and biomass of slugs and snails presented with some natural history information.

Novitsky, Y. I., and Tikhomir, E. V. 1977. Effect of a permanent magnetic field on dry seeds of Vyatka winter rye. *Soviet plant physiology* 24:332–34.

Okigbo, B. N. 1977. Planting into a live mulch. *IFOAM Bulletin* 20.

Painter, R. H. 1951. *Insect resistance in crop plants.* New York: Macmillan Co. (Reprinted 1968, Lawrence, Kansas: University Press of Kansas.)

An excellent source with a phenomenal bibliography.

Patterson, D. D. 1939. *Statistical technique in agricultural research: a simple exposition of practice and procedure in biometry.* New York: McGraw-Hill Book Co.

Pennak, R. W. 1953. *Fresh-water invertebrates of the United States.* New York: Ronald Press Co.

Pessala, R., and Hardh, K. 1977. Mulching in the cultivation of pickling cucumber. *Annales Agriculturae Fenniae* 16:64–71.

Peterson, A. 1948. *Larvae of insects. Part I. Lepidoptera and plant-infesting Hymenoptera.* Ann Arbor, Michigan: Edwards Brothers.

———. 1951. *Larvae of insects. Part II. Coleptera, Diptera, Neuroptera, Siphonaptera, Mecoptera, Trichoptera.* Ann Arbor, Michigan: Edwards Brothers.

Excellent reference sources on immature insects. Although the keys are designed for use with a microscope, many of the illustrations show well-known insect pests.

———. 1964. *Entomological techniques: how to work with insects.* 10th ed. Ann Arbor, Michigan: Edwards Brothers.

Peterson, R. T., and McKenny, M. 1968. *A field guide to the wildflowers of Northeastern and Northcentral North America: a visual approach; arranged by color, form, and detail.* Boston: Houghton Mifflin Co.

Pettygrove, G. S. 1971. (reprinted 1976). *How to perform an agricultural experiment.* Mount Rainer, Maryland: Volunteers in Technical Assistance.

Pfeiffer, E. E. 1976. *Weeds and what they tell.* Springfield, Illinois: Biodynamic Farming & Gardening Association.

Pimentel, D. et al. 1973. Food production and the energy crises. *Science* 182:443–49.

Compares energy inputs for corn culture and yield between the years 1945 and 1970. Concludes that the high energy demand of chemical fertilizers and pesticides must be decreased.

———. 1975. Energy and land constraints in food protein production. *Science* 190:754–61.

———. 1976. Land degradation: effects on food and energy resources. *Science* 194:149–55.

Pittman, U. J. 1963. Magnetism and plant growth: I. Effect on germination and early growth of cereal seeds. *Canadian journal of plant science* 43:513–18.

———. 1965. Magnetism and plant growth: III. Effect on germination and early growth of corn and beans. *Canadian journal of plant science* 45:549–555.

———. 1967. Biomagnetic responses in Kharkov 22 M.C. winter wheat. *Canadian journal of plant science* 47:389–93.

———. 1977. Effects of magnetic seed treatment on yields of barley, wheat, and oats in southern Alberta. *Canadian journal of plant science* 57:37–45.

Polya, L. 1961. Injury by soaking of *Populus alba* seeds. *Nature* 189:159–60.

Purvis, M. J.; Collier, D. C.; and Walls, D. 1964. *Laboratory techniques in botany.* London: Butterworth & Co.

Rappaport, R. A. 1971. The flow of energy in an agricultural society. *Scientific American* 225:117–122, 127–132.

Rateaver, B. and Rateaver, G. 1975. *The organic method primer: a practical explanation.* Pauma Valley, California: published by the authors.

Raw, F. 1959. Estimating earthworm populations by using formalin. *Nature* 184:1661–62.

Reed, L. B., and Webb, R. E. 1975. *Insects and diseases of vegetables in the home garden.* USDA Home and Garden Bulletin no. 380.

Not as complete as the larger books on the same subject and a little heavy on chemical cures, but an inexpensive and handy guide.

Retallack, D. 1973. *The sound of music and plants.* Santa Monica, California: DeVoss & Co.

Reynolds, J. W. 1972. Contributions to North American earthworms (Annelida). no. 2. *Bulletin of the Tall Timbers Research Station,* 11:41–57.

The activity and distribution of earthworms in tulip poplar stands in the Great Smoky Mountains National Park, Sevier County, Tennessee (Acanthodrilidae, Lumbicidae and Magascolecidae).

———. 1977. *The earthworms (Lumbricidae and Sparganophilidae) of Ontario.* Life Sciences Miscellaneous Publications, Royal Ontario Museum (100 Queen's Park, Toronto, ON M5S 2C6 Canada).

Roberts, E. H., ed. 1972. *Viability of seeds.* Syracuse, New York: Syracuse University Press.

Satchell, J. E. 1955. Some aspects of earthworm ecology. Pp. 180–201 *in* D. McKevan, ed. *Soil zoology.* London: Butterworth & Co.

———. 1967. Lubricidae. Pp. 259–322 *in* A. Burges and F. Raw, eds., *Soil biology.* New York: Academic Press.

———. 1969. Methods of sampling earthworm populations. *Pedobiologia* 9:20–25.

———. 1971. "Earthworms" Pp. 107–27 *in* J. Philipson, ed., *Methods of study in quantitative soil ecology: population, production, and energy flow.* International Biological Program Handbook no. 18. Oxford, England: Blackwell Scientific Publications.

Schmeckebier, L. F., and Eastin, R. B. 1969. *Government publications & their use.* rev. ed. Washington, D.C.: Brookings Institution.

Schwartz, P. H., Jr. 1975. *Insects on trees and shrubs around the home.* USDA Agricultural Research Service Home and Garden Bulletin no. 214.

———. 1977. *Control of insects on deciduous fruits and tree nuts in the home orchard—without insecticides.* USDA Home and Garden Bulletin no. 211.

Provides illustrations and descriptions of common pests.

Sheehy, P. et al. 1977. 9th ed. *Guide to reference books*. Chicago: American Library Association. (previous edition edited by C. M. Winchell).

Sidaway, G. H. 1966. Influence of electrostatic field on seed germination. *Nature* 211:303.

Smith, R. C., and Reid, W. M. 1972. 8th ed. *Guide to the literature of the life sciences*. Minneapolis, Minnesota: Burgess Publishing Co.

Snedecor, G. W., and Cochran, W. G. 1967. *Statistical methods*. 6th ed. Ames, Iowa: Iowa State University Press.

Sprague, H. B., ed. 1964. *Hunger signs in crops*. 3d ed. New York: David McKay Co.

Strekova, V. Y. et al. 1965. Some physiological and cytological changes in germinating seeds in a stationary magnetic field: I. The effect on a non-uniform field of low intensity. *Soviet plant physiology* 12:804–12.

Tarakanova, G. A. et al. 1965. Some physiological and cytological changes in germinating seeds in a stationary magnetic field: II. The effect of a uniform magnetic field of low intensity. *Soviet plant physiology* 12:904–11.

Thomas, D. C. 1944. Discussion on slugs. Part II. Field sampling for slugs. *Annals of applied biology* 31:163–64.
  Compares methods of field sampling and presents the use of ammonium sulphate as a barrier valuable in determining the area over which slugs are attracted to food sources.

Townsend, W. N. 1973. *An introduction to the scientific study of the soil*. 5th ed. New York: Saint Martin's Press.

Union list of serials in the libraries of the United States & Canada. 3d ed. 5 vols. 1965. New York: H. W. Wilson Co.

Usinger, R. L., ed. 1956. *Aquatic insects of California with keys to North American genera and California species*. Berkeley, California: Univ. of California Press.

Van Vliet, L. J. P.; Wall, G. J.; and Dickonson, W. T. 1976. Effects of agricultural land use on potential sheet erosion losses in southern Ontario. *Canadian journal of the soil* 56:443–51.

Von Frisch, K. 1971. *Bees: their vision, chemical senses, & language*. 2d ed. Ithaca, New York: Cornell Univ. Press.
  A pleasure and an inspiration.

Walford, A. J. 1975. *Guide to reference material.* 3d ed. vol. 1. Science and Technology. London: Library Association.

Walsh, L. M., and Beaton, J. D., eds. 1973. *Soil testing and plant analysis.* Madison, Wisconsin: Soil Science Society of America.

Watt, B. K., and Merrill, A. L. 1963. *Composition of foods: raw, processed, prepared.* Agriculture Handbook 8. Washington, D.C.: USDA Consumer and Food Economics Research Division.

Weaver, J. E., and Clements, F. E. 1938. *Plant ecology.* 2d ed. New York: McGraw-Hill Book Co.

Discusses vegetative indicators of different soil types and contains a wealth of information on plant ecology.

Weinberger, P., and Measures, M. 1968. The effect of two audible sound frequencies on the germination and growth of spring and winter wheat. *Canadian journal of botany* 46:1151–58.

Westcott, Cynthia, ed. 1960. *Handbook on biological control of plant pests.* Special printing of *Plants and gardens* (16:3). Brooklyn, New York: Brooklyn Botanic Garden.

Descriptions of insects used for biological control and discussions of biological control programs.

———. 1973. *The gardener's bug book.* 4th ed. New York: Doubleday & Co.

Describes specific pests found in the garden.

Whyte, R. O. 1958. Plant exploration, collection, and introduction. FAO Agricultural Studies no. 41. Rome, Italy.

Yates, F. 1933. The analysis of replicated experiments when the field results are incomplete. *Empire journal of experimental agriculture* 1:129–42.

Yearbook of Agriculture. 1936. *Better plants and animals: a survey of superior germ plasm.* Washington, D.C.: USDA.

———. 1938. *Soils and men.* Washington, D.C.: USDA.

———. 1952. *Insects.* Washington, D.C.: USDA.

———. 1961. *Seeds.* Washington, D.C.: USDA.

Young, M.; Young, H. C.; and Kruzas, A. T. 1977. *Directory of special libraries and information centers.* 2 vols. Detroit: Gale Research Co.

Index

A

Abraham, George and Katy, 8
Abstracts, of periodical
    literature, 27–31
Acetic ether, to kill insects,
    150
Agribusiness, research by, 12
Agway Seed Department, 231
Air, needed in soil, 44
Alcohol, rubbing
    for insect storage, 163
    to kill earthworms, 173
    to kill insects, 151–52
    for plant preservation, 64
Allolobophora earthworms,
    characteristics of, 174
Amaranth, research with, 8
American Horticultural
    Society, 232
Ammonium sulfate, as slug
    barrier, 132
Analysis, of results, 210–26
    confidence intervals for
        success, 223–25
    standard deviation,
        212–13
    statistical symbols,
        211–12
    tabulating data, 210–12
    writing report, 225–26

Aphid
rating infestation of, 207
    rosy apple, 138
Aporrectodea earthworms,
    characteristics of, 175
Apple maggot, 155
Ashes, as insect repellent, 168

B

Background information,
    16–36
    evaluation of, 34–36
    keeping research log,
        17–18
    sources of, 26–27
        government documents,
        31–33
        library, 18–19
        periodicals, 27–31
        personal contact, 33–34
Beer, as slug bait, 131
Beetles
    elm bark, 159
    killing of, 151
Bibliography of Agriculture,
    33
Bimastos earthworms,
    characteristics of, 176

Index

Biodynamic/French Intensive
method of agriculture,
179
Blackflies, trapping of, 158
Blight, of American chestnut,
7, 14–15
Bolting cloth, for insect
collection net, 146
Books, reference, use of,
19–21
Books in Print, 26
Bran, as slug bait, 131
Bromfield, Louis, 184–85
Brooklyn Botanical Gardens,
chestnut research by,
15
Brookstone Company, as
supplies source, 228
Brushes, watercolor, for
handling insects, 147
Butterflies, killing of, 151

C

Calcium cyanide. *See*
Cyanide
Calgon water softener, for
sedimentation soil
test, 46
Call numbers, of books, 22
Calorie, definition of, 123
Card catalog, use of, 19–25
Carolina Biological Supply
Company, 228
Carrot rust fly, 138
Castanea. See Chestnut,
American
Cattails, as soil quality
indicator, 54

Chamomile, as soil quality
indicator, 54
Chestnut, American, research
with, 7–8, 14–5
Chickweed, as living mulch,
187
Cigarette lighter fluid, to kill
insects, 151
Cinquefoil, as soil quality
indicator, 56
Clay, 50
feel of, 49
*Climatological Data of the
United States
Weather Bureau*, 40
Collection net, for catching
insects, 145–46
Color perception, of insects,
157
Companion planting,
experimenting with,
11
Competition, between plants,
effect on behavior,
72–73
Compost
experimentation with, 9
as soil equalizer, 69
Correlation, definition of, 3
Corn, in low-tillage farming,
184–85
Cost efficiency, calculating of,
221
County cooperative extension
office, soil testing by,
44
Cover crop
as living mulch, 187
used with low-tillage,
184, 185

249